Wonder WOMEN

25 INNOVATORS, INVENTORS, AND
TRAILBLAZERS WHO CHANGED HISTORY

WONDER WOMEN

Written by **SAM MAGGS**

Illustrated by **SOPHIA FOSTER-DIMINO**

QUIRK BOOKS
PHILADELPHIA

This book is dedicated to all the brave, strong, rule-breaking, expectation-flouting, wild women throughout history who made it possible for me to be here today, writing something like this. We owe you everything.

And to Nancy, Karyn, Elena, Soha, Meg, Rachel, Danny, Emma, Kristin, Jill, Becky, Maria, Blair, and all the other wonder women in my life. You inspire me every day.

Library of Congress Cataloging in Publication Number: 2016930951

ISBN: 978-1-59474-925-4

Printed in China
Typeset in Nanami Rounded and Sabon

Designed by Andie Reid
Illustrations by Sophia Foster-Dimino
Production management by John J. McGurk

Quirk Books
215 Church Street
Philadelphia, PA 19106
quirkbooks.com

10 9 8 7 6 5 4 3 2 1

Contents

CHAPTER THREE:
WOMEN OF ESPIONAGE

CHAPTER FOUR:
WOMEN OF INNOVATION

CHAPTER FIVE:
WOMEN OF ADVENTURE

INTRODUCTION

We Can Do It!

Representation is important.

Media critics use this phrase all the time. We say it to drive home the point that everyone—no matter their gender, sexuality, race, ability, or any part of their identity—deserves to see characters like them on the page and onscreen. Why? Because when media is full of diverse heroes, every gal will unconsciously learn that she too can be the star of the story, that "hero" status isn't reserved for people who look like Superman, that she's not stuck as a damsel in distress. If she wants to foil the enemy or save the day or rescue herself, she can.

But something we often forget is that representation matters *everywhere*, not just in fiction but also in our everyday IRL lives. The bummer is that although we're making significant strides in the media, the same cannot yet be said for the office or the classroom. Lack of representation is why, when I ask you to think of a scientist, the first person who comes to mind is a white-jacketed, messy-haired man. It's why women's historical impact is traditionally explored in an optional course called Women's Studies, whereas compulsory classes on the historical impact of men are simply called History. It's why only 30 percent of employees at Google are women, only 22 percent of game developers are women, only 5 percent of

U.S. patents include a woman's name. In this kind of social climate, it's easy to grow up thinking that women don't get involved in tech or science or medicine or engineering, because who among us really ever has?

Of course, awesome, accomplished, successful women have existed since humans started painting on stones with their extremities. Yet somehow we never seem to hear about these noteworthy heroines. Did you know that 80 percent of all code breakers during World War II were female? (You wouldn't know it from Hollywood, considering that Keira Knightley was the only lady in *The Imitation Game*.) How about that the paper bag your take-out comes in was invented by a woman? Or the process that made the shirt on your back possible? Or the first computer program, or wireless tech, or nuclear fission? What about all the pioneering women around the globe who—despite a dearth of access to education, money, tools, or, you know, *freedom*—busted their butts and their brains in the face of great odds to become the first lady doctors, mountaineers, super spies, or field biologists?

What about Anandibai Joshi, who crossed an ocean alone to help advance women's health in her native India? Or Jacqueline Felicie de Almania, a medieval doctor dragged to court for daring to be better than her male colleagues? The more I researched for this book, the more I knew these women's stories had to be told for the good of all humans everywhere. History is full of lady engineers and spies and scientists. But history is also written by the victorious, and it may not surprise you that thus far the overwhelming winners have been straight white dudes. That hasn't worked out so well for everyone else.

The good news is that we can fix this problem, tipping the scales to be a bit better balanced. It's time to stop accepting women's role in history as limited to keeping a great home (though admittedly a harder job than it looks!) and birthing the dudes we learn about in art history or religion or biology class. It's time to shake off the bogus fear that pursuing any interest that falls outside the traditionally "feminine"—say, working in a STEM field, exploring the world, designing a video game—will make us complete pariahs. It's time for women to take our place in a long line of brilliant, patriarchy-smashing, butt-kicking chicks.

First, though, we have to get the stories of these women out into the world. Because *representation matters.* And we ladies need real inspiration for the next time we find ourselves doubting our ability to invent something, the next time we fear learning how to code, the next time we feel like we just don't belong.

So join me on a journey into the history of bad-as-heck babes. Just keep in mind that these are only some of the amazing women in the history of our world. Many more are out there, and many more are to come. In fact, you know what?

You're next.

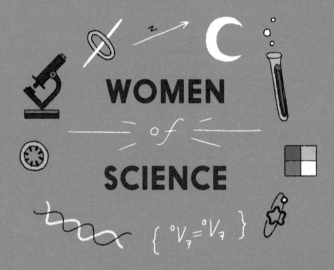

CHAPTER ONE

WOMEN
of
SCIENCE

$\{\,^\circ V_7 = \,^\circ V_7\,\}$

Did you know that a woman named Rosalind Franklin was instrumental in the discovery of DNA, instead of only those two guys you read about in your chem text? Or that, in 1974, the Nobel Prize in physics was awarded to Jocelyn Bell Burnell's male supervisor after *she* discovered pulsars? It's true. The world has been and continues to be filled with radical lady astronomers, biologists, physicists, programmers, and more, and we are way overdue to bask in their greatness. So let's right some of history's wrongs by delving into the fascinating lives of the most sensational, and crucial, women in science, technology, engineering, and math (aka STEM, for the uninitiated. Consider yourself initiated!).

Wang ZHENYI

1768–1797

CHINESE ASTRONOMER,
MATHEMATICIAN, AND POET

During the late 1700s, women in China were expected to do what women just about everywhere at that time were expected to do: sew, cook, have babies, and perhaps sew a little more for good measure. Writing politically charged texts was out of the question, especially since any Chinese person—woman or man—risked severe punishment for criticizing the emperor. A woman who managed to publish social tracts in such a repressive climate would have to Not Give a Dang, which Wang Zhenyi definitely didn't. Paying no regard to the danger that she could be chopped to bits for her pursuits, or that she would have been deemed unmarriageable (the horror!), she published her opinions anyway and became one of the best-known scientists and poets of her time.

Zhenyi (Wang was her family name) was born into feudal China during the height of the Qing dynasty (1644–1911/12), China's last imperial rulership. At the time, the country was dealing with not only an unsustainable population boom but also the devastating Sino-Burmese War, wherein China was trying to take over Burma. The Qianlong Emperor, as the dynasty's fourth ruler was known, was all about preserving Confucian culture (which prized humanistic values like compassion and loyalty, putting a high value on acting ethically and morally in everyday life), and so he built up the imperial collection, which included art, historical documents, and rare books. But like most people with absolute power, the emperor took things a *little* too far, sliding easily from literary appreciation to literary persecution if he didn't like what you were layin' down, art-wise—book burning, beheadings, slowly slicing writers and artists into pieces until they died painfully, the usual.

Zhenyi was well-off (a situation that helps just about everyone in every era), but the Wang family was in decline. Her grandfather was a former governor, and the family home near present-day Nanjing, in eastern China, housed his epic library of over seventy-five bookshelves (Hogwarts-sized for the Qing dynasty). Growing up, Zhenyi took it upon herself to read her way through her grandfather's entire collection, and somehow she also managed to find time to study equestrian arts and archery with the wife of a Mongolian general (because apparently being a self-taught genius at math and science just wasn't enough). Zhenyi *knew* she was awesome, too. In one of her well-regarded poems, she writes that her ambition was "to a kind even stronger than a man's" and that she was often "reluctant to ride a horse with make-up" (totally understandable since eyeliner back then was probably not smudge-proof).

After an impressive childhood of self-education, a teenaged Zhenyi traveled extensively with her father throughout China, witnessing firsthand many of the problems from which the country was suffering. The population had grown so quickly that there weren't enough resources to go around, and so impoverished and hungry people began fighting over scarce farmland while the rich remained indifferent and unaffected. Agonized by the plight of her country's version of the 99 percent, Zhenyi expressed her feelings in a series of poems about injustice (since Twitter had yet to be invented). These poems weren't written in the kind of dainty, flowery language common to most female poets of the time. Instead, they were unsparing descriptions of the massive inequity between China's classes:

Village is empty of cooking smoke,
Rich families let grains stored decay;
In wormwood strewed pitiful starved bodies,
Greedy officials yet push farm levying.

(*Burn!*)

Zhenyi's protest poetry wasn't just a hobby. It led her to befriend and exchange ideas with other ahead-of-their-time lady scholars in both nearby Jiangning and countrywide. Zhenyi even named herself Jiangning Nüshi, meaning "female intellectual from Jiangning"—perhaps not the most creative name, sure, but she was about to earn the title in a big way. At that time in China, many astronomical principles were still revolutionary (for comparison, some guys in England were just starting to figure out what *that whole Milky Way thing* was all about). But sharp-eyed Zhenyi stood on the cutting edge, writing papers describing the equinoxes; the rotation of the sun, moon, and planets; trigonometry and the Pythagorean theorem; and the fact that the Earth was round and we weren't going to fall off its edge anytime soon. Her most ground-breaking publication was a treatise titled *The Explanation of a Lunar Eclipse*—the first on the subject that anybody in Zhenyi's neck of the woods had ever written. To prove her theory, Zhenyi went into a garden and set down a round table (representing the Earth), hung a lamp above it (the sun), and stuck a round mirror on one side of the table (the moon). Then she moved the three objects the way their corresponding celestial bodies move and *bam!*—proof of a lunar eclipse worthy of any modern science fair. When many others blamed the eclipse phenomenon on supernatural events, Zhenyi wrote back, "Actually, it's definitely because of the moon." (Direct quote!)

All of Zhenyi's fancy research didn't detract from her passion to reach people at every level of the social hierarchy. She knew that not everyone had the same access to books and education as she did (she also realized that a lot of the men who published scientific papers and math theorems before her were really bad at it), so she spread the Joy of Science by rewriting old arcane texts into simple language and republished them for beginners—and that's on *top* of all the books she was writing on her own. Basically, Zhenyi was the Bill Nye of eighteenth-century China. She would totally be hosting *Cosmos* were she alive today.

And all that stuff about being "unmarriageable"? Zhenyi soon found a rad dude who loved her for who she was (because who wouldn't?) and tied the knot at age twenty-five. Marriage didn't slow her down any, though; she remained a constant and outspoken advocate for equality of both the classes and the sexes. In one of her texts, Zhenyi decries that the majority of her compatriots in Qing dynasty China felt "women should only do cooking and sewing" because, in her words, men and women "are all people who have the same reason for studying." (Darn right, Zhenyi. Can you shout that a little louder into the twenty-first century?)

Though she lived to only twenty-nine years old, she achieved over 300,000% of an average human's scientific accomplishments and left the world a better and smarter place, all while advancing the position of women in eighteenth-century China. And as for that daughters-being-heroic thing? I, for one, am totally convinced.

Ada LOVELACE

1815–
1852

BRITISH MATHEMATICIAN
AND PROGRAMMER

"This science constitutes the language through which alone we can adequately express the great facts of the natural world."

he next time an online troll tries to tell you coding isn't for girls, just think of Ada Lovelace. As the creator of the first-ever computer program, Ada is the reason that, if anything, coding has *always* been for girls.

Born Augusta Ada King in 1815, this future numerical nerd was the only legitimate child of Lord Byron, the famous Romantic poet/lovable eccentric. (You know the guy: he wrote *Don Juan* and *Childe Harold* and traveled around Europe allegedly gettin' *real friendly* with his half sister before eventually trying to take over Greece. There's a reason we call tempestuous bros Byronic.) Ada's mother, Anne, was a mathematician in her own right, and despite Lord Byron praising Anne as the "Princess of Parallelograms," the two had a tumultuous relationship and young Ada never really met her father.

Now picture Georgian-Regency London of 1815: Napoleon had finally surrendered to England; the divide between rich and poor was epic; Jane Austen had just published *Emma*; empire waists were the hottest fashion; and the prince regent was sponsoring many artists and architects, leading to a kind of mini cultural renaissance. But Anne, worried that Ada would turn out like her father, refused to let her daughter anywhere near poetry or the arts. Instead, Ada was to study math and science. Frequently ill as a child (in part because her mom was really into the medical practice of using leeches as cure-alls, which, don't do this), Ada spent a lot of time indoors reading and studying. At the tender age of twelve, she designed a pair of mechanical wings after deciding that she wanted to fly. (Did she basically invent steampunk? Can someone credit her for that on Wikipedia?)

But Ada's independence didn't sit right with her mother. Upon discovering that her eighteen-year-old daughter was having an affair with her tutor, Anne shipped Ada off to the British court. Ada's brains and beauty made her instantly popular among royals and courtiers alike, and though she did eventually marry a baron (with whom she had three kids), she continued to indulge in decidedly unladylike pastimes like gambling and party-going (heck yes). She had some close scrapes with misfortune (including a failed mathematical model for successful horse-racing predictions that left Ada hugely in debt) and indulged in unusual obsessions (i.e., fairies and the "unseen worlds around us"), but eventually her mom's left-brainedness balanced out Ada's Byronic side. Soon Ada was calling herself an "Analyst (& Metaphysician)," studying "poetical science," and publishing papers about how the brain creates thoughts and how music relates to math.

But her papers were only the beginning. In 1833 Ada met Charles Babbage, a mathematician who, a decade earlier, had invented a computer—essentially a giant mechanical calculator—called the Difference Engine (which would be a great name for an all-girl EDM band, if you're looking to start one). He also envisioned a more advanced computer/calculator called the Analytical Engine. Where the Difference Engine was relegated to "computing and printing tables of mathematical functions by addition," the new Analytical Engine would include subtraction, multiplication, and division, and "plans called for programming it with punched cards."

Ada (whom Babbage adorably called the "Enchantress of Numbers" and "Lady Fairy") jumped at the chance to study his creation, and in 1843 she published her own notes on the prototype—notes that included a specific algorithm that, using punch cards, could likely teach the engine how to calculate a specific sequence of signed rational numbers known as the Bernoulli numbers. Had Babbage's machine ever come into being, we now know that Ada's idea would have executed flawlessly. And if a "series of instructions that produce a specific outcome from a machine" sounds a lot like a computer program, that's because *it is*—making Ada the first-ever computer programmer.

But Ada wasn't just good with math and problem-solving— she was also a visionary. At the time, everyone was pretty sure that Babbage's engines were good for one thing and one thing only: crunching numbers. Even their inventor thought so. Only Ada, with her poetic insight, was able to predict that, hey, maybe these computer-machines might one day be able to do more. As she noted: "Again, it might act upon other things besides number. . . . Supposing, for instance, that the fundamental relations of pitched sounds in the science of harmony and of musical composition were susceptible of such expression and adaptations, the engine might compose elaborate and scientific pieces of music of any degree of complexity or extent." In other words, she was the first person ever to theorize the potential importance of computers, though she was positive they could never "*originate* anything" and were ultimately incapable of thinking for themselves (which, for the sake of humanity, let's hope she got right).

Unfortunately, we'll never know what great achievements lay ahead for Ada, as she died from uterine cancer at age thirty-six. But she left behind a great legacy: her notes influenced Alan Turing's work in the 1940s on the first legit computers. Of course, in recent years some historians have suggested that Babbage wrote the engine program, not Ada. (If you learn anything from this book, it's that pretty much *no* women's successes have ever gone without being attributed to a man.) Still, glimmers of recognition do shine. Today, the U.S. Department of Defense has a computer language named Ada in her honor, and there's even an Ada Lovelace Day celebrated every October 13, a time to raise the profile of women in STEM and encourage a new generation of "number enchantresses." We're coding in your honor, Ada.

Lise
MEITNER

1878–
1968

AUSTRIAN NUCLEAR PHYSICIST

Men have long taken credit for the work of smart women. We're striving to correct much of that false history, but it's difficult, if not impossible, to fully make it up to the many female scientists shafted by the historic record in favor of their male colleagues. If that kind of affront makes you angry, then get ready to have some major feelings about Lise Meitner, the most important scientist of the twentieth century you've probably never heard of.

Born in Vienna in 1878, Lise was the third of eight children. In a stroke of enlightened thinking, her father insisted that all his children receive the same educational opportunities regardless of gender. Lise loved learning all the things, later saying she showed a "marked bent" for physics as a child, a preference that continued into adulthood. After becoming one of the first women to earn a doctoral degree in physics from the University of Vienna in 1905 (often finding herself the only woman in a class of a hundred students), Lise teamed up with the chemist Otto Hahn, who would eventually help her make beautiful scientific discoveries but would also royally screw her over.

When Lise began researching alongside Otto in the radio-chemistry department at the Kaiser-Wilhelm Institute, the going got a whole lot tougher on our gal than it already had been. Lise was relegated to the status of "guest" and denied a salary because her boss didn't want women in the lab for fear that their "rather exotic hairstyle" might catch fire from a Bunsen burner (unlike a man's bushy beard?). Lise was instead forced to set up their lab in a carpentry shop in the basement. And lest you think the sexism was limited to that particular lab, Lise once had an article rejected from the encyclopedia *Brockhaus* when the editor discovered her given name (she'd previously published multiple times under her last name) because "he would not think of printing an article written by a woman." It was only in 1913 that Lise started being paid for her work, after a university in Prague offered her an assistant professorship. When World War I hit the next year, Lise took a quick break from science to become an X-ray technician—and since we know that Einstein used to call her Germany's own Marie Curie, it seems pretty certain she rocked at radiation, too.

After returning to her lab in 1917, Lise was ready to just get on with stuff and do the science—and *did she ever.* She discovered a stable form of the element protactinium (along with a bunch of other isotopes) and finally, a year later, was offered her own radioactive physics department at the Kaiser-Wilhelm Institute. Then in 1922 Lise discovered the atomic phenomenon that causes emissions from the surface of electrons, which is now called the Auger effect, after the French guy who "discovered" the exact same thing two years later (noticing a trend?). Oh, and Lise also became Germany's first female physics professor, although the press laughed and called her inaugural speech "cosmetic physics" instead of "cosmic physics." (Get it? Because she's a lady and ladies like makeup! *Hilarious.*) Despite much evidence to the contrary, no one was buying the notion that gals could be good at sciencing, but Lise refused to let that fly. As she would later say, "The gradual development of the professional and legal equality of women can only be properly understood if one remembers how many accepted customs had to be overcome in the struggle for the emancipation of women."

Fast-forward to 1930s Berlin, when Lise was fifty-nine years old and Nazism was on the rise. Otto was safe, but Lise had Jewish parentage, so despite initially believing she'd be left alone because she was "too valuable to annoy," she realized she was in danger. She got the heck out of Germany with only two small suitcases and ten deutsche marks to her name. Her escape was orchestrated by a group of scientists that included Good Guy Scientist Niels Bohr, who would later go on to champion Lise's work and nominate her for three Nobel Prizes (way to not be a jerk, Niels!).

After her dramatic flight (which Otto casually attributed to—and this is a direct quote—"these Hitler regime things"), Lise set up shop in Stockholm at the lab of a guy named Manne Siegbahn. Now Manne, unlike Good Guy Niels, hated women in the sciences (and was therefore kind of a trashbag). He refused to give Lise collaborators, equipment, tech support, or even her own set of keys to the lab, and he paid her an assistant's measly salary. (Lise would later write that in searching for "male supporters of the higher education of women and of their professional equality with men, then it is remarkable how few men of general reputation we find." No kidding.) Despite these setbacks (and the misery and loneliness that accompanied fleeing her homeland), Lise continued to work, writing back and forth with Otto about a little thing she had been considering: how to split the nuclear atom into smaller parts, also known as nuclear fission. Yeah—kind of a big deal.

After years of research and correspondence, Otto followed Lise's instructions and bombarded some uranium with neutrons. At this point, Otto wrote a nice letter to Lise that basically said, "I smacked uranium with neutrons and barium came out? Don't understand? Halp???" (What he really wrote was: "Perhaps you can suggest some sort of fantastic explanation. We knew ourselves that [uranium] can't really break up into barium . . . so try and think of some other possibility." Which is equally as clueless, but still.) So Lise wrote him a nice explanatory letter (after, some sources romantically claim, drawing calculations in the Swedish snow on a Christmas hike with her physicist nephew, as if her life was a scene out of *A Beautiful Mind*), making her the first-ever person on the planet to accurately articulate what happens to atoms during nuclear fission. But since Lise was exiled from Germany, Otto published *their* findings and *Lise's theory* in the journal *Nature*—without giving Lise credit in the byline or the text. Then in 1944, despite Lise having coined the term *nuclear fission* in her own *Nature* article in 1939, Otto won the Nobel Prize in chemistry for the discovery, even though his original note to Lise promised that they "would be together in this work after all." Although his 1946 Nobel lecture did mention Lise five times, most people assumed she was merely Otto's junior assistant, a misconception that he seems to have done nothing to correct.

Meanwhile, Lise was using her powers for good—or *not* using them, as it happened. She turned down an invitation to work on the Manhattan Project and refused to have anything to do with the nuclear bomb, becoming horrified, as you can imagine, at what her Big Discovery had made possible. Lise hoped that "the atomic bomb will make humanity realize that we must, once and for all, be done with war." Unfortunately, as we all know, war didn't end because of her work—and neither did sexism. At a presidential dinner celebrating a "Woman of the Year" award bestowed upon Lise in 1946, U.S. president Harry Truman greeted her as "the little lady who got us into all of this!" (which she just *loved*). When the MGM film company showed her a script for a biopic of her life, she hated that it was based on "the stupid newspaper story that I left Germany with the bomb in my purse." Despite an increased offer from the studio, she declared that she "would rather walk naked down Broadway" than see the film produced.

Lise would go on to lecture around the world, receive a butt-load of honorary degrees and scientific honors, and have a crater on the moon, a crater on Venus, and an asteroid named after her. She died in Cambridge, England, at the age of eighty-nine.

Today, a growing number of people are recognizing Lise's instrumental work in discovering nuclear fission. In fact, element 109 is named meitnerium in her honor (and I'm pretty sure there's no element called hahnium, so take that). Lise's life was definitely not easy, but she lived it to the fullest. Wish granted, lady.

Emmy
NOETHER

1882–1935

GERMAN MATHEMATICIAN
AND PHYSICIST

> *"My methods are really methods of*
> *working and thinking; this is why they*
> *have crept in everywhere anonymously."*

Now, I know that "praise from a bunch of men" isn't exactly the most important criterion for determining the value of a lady's accomplishments, but when the genius mathematicians Pavel Alexandrov, Jean Dieudonné, Hermann Weyl, Norbert Wiener, and Albert Einstein *all* say that someone is the most important woman in the history of math, chances are they're not wrong. The woman in question? Emmy Noether.

Amalie Emmy Noether was a total BAMF from the beginning. Born in 1882 to the German mathematician Max Noether and his wife, Ida, Emmy received an early education typical for girls at the time—studying mostly music and dance—and in 1900 went on to finishing school, where she passed her exams with flying colors. She initially intended to become an English and French teacher, but when the University of Erlangen began (reluctantly) allowing women through its doors (even though administrators feared that doing so would "overthrow all academic order," which I guess is German for "upset all the men"), Emmy signed up for some math classes—and turned out to be *really, really* good at them. At first she could only audit courses, and even then she had to obtain the permission of each professor. But she kept at it and graduated in 1903. Once the restrictions against female students had been eliminated,

Emmy was able to undertake her dissertation, which she completed in 1907. (It's titled "On the Complete Systems of Invariants for Ternary Biquadratic Forms," which sounds like super-breezy reading, no?). She would later call her paper a "*Formelngestrüpp*" and "*Mist*" (that's "jungle of formulas" and "crap") because Emmy was self-deprecating and likable, sort of a twentieth-century German Zooey Deschanel, complete with quirky bow tie.

But even with the restrictions lifted against women in universities, do you think guy scholars were okay with a woman trying to work in their (well, "their") math departments, as though she *belonged*? Nope. Grudgingly, the men did let Emmy work at the university for seven years—but for *zero salary*. (And we think summer internships are rough!) Even when her hard work paid off and she was invited in 1915 to join the University of Göttingen as a lecturer, the administration made her lecture for four more years under the name of her male supervisor.

That's how much Emmy loved math: she did her thing *for free* under humiliating circumstances. (How can you not be blown away by her dedication?) Fortunately, Emmy's supervisor was ahead of his time. He didn't understand why his colleagues were so against her and campaigned to get Emmy a real post at the university. "I do not see that the sex of a candidate is an argument against her admission as [an official lecturer]," he said. "After all, we are a university, not a bathhouse." (Snap!) Emmy in turn took that statement as a challenge and started swimming at a men-only pool. (Double snaps!)

Finally, in 1919 Emmy began to lecture under her own banner, and mathematicians around the world soon took notice—especially since she proved some important theorems around this time. How important? Potentially *the* most important. Noether's theorem (which we do *not* have the page space to write out in its entirety, trust us) basically explains that energy can neither be created nor destroyed. It's why a bicycle works the way it does: because a spinning symmetrical bicycle wheel will always want to maintain its original direction and speed. Emmy's theorem (which is technically *four* theorems) has been called one of "the most important mathematical theorems ever" by modern physicists and is essentially as important as Einstein's theory of relativity (a little supposition you may have heard of). The theorem put Emmy's name on the map, literally. By 1933 people were calling her students "Noether boys," and these days all objects that meet the qualifications of her theorem are called "Noetherian." (Namecheck? Check.)

But not everything was easy: this was 1930s Germany after all, and Emmy was Jewish. When the Nazis threw Jewish scholars out of universities, Emmy escaped to the United States and eventually settled in Pennsylvania, where she took a post at Bryn Mawr College in 1933. There she befriended fellow lady mathematician Anna Wheeler and was praised by the college president as an awesome example for mathematicians everywhere. Though Emmy also lectured at Princeton's Flexner Institute, she found it to be a "men's university, where nothing female [was] admitted," and decided to stick it out at Bryn Mawr. Continuing her lifelong independent streak, Emmy, who was near-sighted and spoke with a lisp, never married, wore men's shoes, and was overwhelmingly optimistic— fellow mathematician Hermann Weyl once described her as "warm like a loaf of bread." One day during a lecture break when two female students approached her to (hopefully politely) point out her eccentric appearance (including frizzy hair and untucked shirt), they couldn't even get their professor's attention because Emmy was too busy with other students discussing *more math.*

In 1935 Emmy underwent surgery for an ovarian cyst and died from complications four days later, at the age of fifty-three. Albert Einstein wrote a eulogy, published in the *New York Times,* in which he called her "the most significant creative mathematical genius thus far produced since the higher education of women began." Hermann Weyl gave a moving memorial address, praising Emmy as "a great mathematician, the greatest, I firmly believe, that her sex has ever produced, and a great woman." Today, Emmy has a crater on the moon *and* an asteroid named after her, and she's even graced the Google Doodle. So thanks, Emmy. The next generation of brilliant math ladies will have so much to say about you.

Alice
BALL

1892–
1916

AMERICAN CHEMIST
AND MEDICAL RESEARCHER

"Oil from the seed [of the chaulmoogra tree (Hydnocarpus)] was used to relieve symptoms of leprosy. Alice A. Ball—African-American College of Hawai'i instructor, research chemist, and the first woman to receive a master's degree from the College of Hawai'i (Class of 1915)—extracted the oil's active ingredient in the 1910's."

I f you love science and equality but hate leprosy (and who doesn't?), Alice Ball is 100 percent your kind of gal. As a young scientist, she not only overcame a hugely prejudiced environment to pursue an education, but she also achieved the kind of life-saving research breakthroughs that much older scientists would envy—and steal.

Before she rocked her research, Alice Ball was born in the late nineteenth century to a family of pioneers in Seattle, Washington. Her grandfather had been an abolitionist and one of the first African American men to learn how to create daguerreotypes (an early form of photography and *not* something that steampunk authors made up). Her father was a lawyer and editor of the *Colored Citizen* newspaper, and her mother was a well-regarded photographer of Black leaders. After becoming interested in the chemicals used to develop photographs (and acing all her high school classes), Alice attended the University of Washington to study science, earning not one but *two* bachelor's degrees: in pharmaceutical chemistry and science. In 1914, as a twenty-two-year-old undergrad, Alice copublished an eleven-page article in the *Journal of the American Chemical Society* titled "Benzoylations in Ether Solution," which featured tons of smart-person observations, such as "Since the balance was sensitive to only 0.05mg it is evident that errors of weight alone account fully for the surprisingly small variations observed." Ace!

All that work is impressive by anyone's standards at any time in history, but we're talking about the early 1900s, when racial discrimination was rampant (and legal) in much of the United States and only about 2,300 of Seattle's 81,000 residents were Black. In 1910, the year Alice entered college, 84 percent of Black female professionals in Seattle worked as domestic servants. So it's safe to say that she not only rocked at chemistry, but she did so in spite of what society *thought* she could do. Offered scholarships at both Berkeley and the University of Hawai'i, Alice chose the latter, having family history in the Pacific Islands. By 1915 she was the first woman *and* the first African American to graduate with a master's degree from the University of Hawai'i, and she subsequently took a teaching position that made her the university's first Black professor of chemistry.

While working on her thesis (on the chemical makeup of awa root, or kava, a sedative plant), Alice was approached by Harry T. Hollmann, an assistant surgeon and U.S. public health officer at nearby Kalihi Hospital. Hollmann was seeking a more effective treatment for Hansen's disease (aka leprosy, an infection that causes debilitating and contagious skin lesions). Never one to back down from a challenge, Alice agreed to help and started researching the properties of an ingredient called chaulmoogra oil. In Indian and Chinese medicine, oil made from seeds of the chaulmoogra tree had long been used to treat skin diseases like leprosy and eczema. Unfortunately, the oil wasn't super effective when applied topically, and it tasted too horrible for anyone to be willing to ingest it. Injections of the substance were painful, since its active ingredients (chaulmoogric acid and hydnocarpic acid) are insoluble in water (and thus in humans); unpleasant side effects further reduced the appeal of this treatment method. But chemistry wizard Alice fixed the problem:

by isolating the ethyl esters of the fatty acids present in the oil, she made the treatment injectable. And she accomplished this amazing feat at the age of only *twenty-three*.

Before she was able to publish her results, Alice fell ill after accidentally inhaling chlorine gas during a lab demonstration of gas masks. After traveling to Seattle for treatment, she resumed teaching for a few months before dying on December 31, 1916, at age twenty-four, likely from aftereffects of the accident. (I say "likely" because her death certificate has since been altered to report tuberculosis as the cause of death, although a 1917 newspaper article reported that she died of chlorine poisoning.) Fortunately, Alice's death was not in vain; her injectable treatment for Hansen's disease would save seventy-eight patients at Kalihi Hospital and countless more across the world. It remained the primary treatment for leprosy for three decades, until the invention of sulfone drugs in the 1940s. And so, in honor of its inventor, Alice Ball, the ethyl ester isolation process was named . . . the Dean Method.

Yes, after Alice's untimely death, University of Hawai'i president Dr. Arthur Dean began creating large quantities of the injectable oil for use in treatment, and then he went on to take all the credit for the therapy. But the method was completely Alice's: according to University of Hawai'i professor Kathryn Takara: "[Ball] really did all the research. The Ball Method became [Dean's] method." To his credit, Dr. Hollmann *did* try to name Alice as the method's inventor in a 1922 paper titled "The Fatty Acids of Chaulmoogra Oil in the Treatment of Leprosy and Other Diseases," wherein he says of Dean's Method: "I cannot see that there is any improvement over the original technic as worked out by Miss Ball." Hollmann adds that Alice, "an instructress in chemistry," was the one who "solved the problem," and he calls the solution "Ball's Method." The media picked up on it, too. A brief 1925 article in the *Honolulu Advertiser* describes Ball as a "Hawai'ian Girl Heroine."

Despite these valiant efforts, the University of Hawai'i and the rest of the world essentially forgot about Alice for a century. Then in 2000 the school attached a plaque inscribed with her name to the campus's only chaulmoogra tree (aw!) and awarded her a medal of distinction. Hawai'i also now recognizes Alice Ball Day on February 29 (a date that gives you a nice four-year interval to plan a huge bash between celebrations). Today, two activist scholars are to be thanked for Alice's restored legacy: Dr. Takara, who discovered her in the University of Hawai'i archives in 1977; and a federal retiree in Baltimore named Stan Ali, who accidentally found mention of "young Negro chemist, Alice Ball," while reading Charles Dutton's 1932 book on leprosy, *The Samaritans of Molokai*. Not only did Ali's research into Alice's history lead directly to her University of Hawai'i honors, but he also wants to rename the university's Dean Hall in her honor (or at least get a lab named after her), given that Dean was so clearly "guilty of plagiarism." After all the work that Alice did in her twenty-four short years, she clearly deserves it.

CHEMISTS, SCHOLARS, <u>AND</u> STARGAZING PHILOSOPHERS

Other Amazing Women of Science

HYPATIA

CA. 350/70–415 One of the baddest babes of the first millennium, Hypatia became head of the University of Alexandria's Neoplatonist School at just thirty years old, teaching the male students philosophy, math, and physics. Despite living in Christian-controlled Egypt, Hypatia continued to practice her Hellenistic pagan ways and pulled off lots of other rebellious acts, like driving her own chariot, wearing teacher's clothes instead of traditional women's garb, and preaching philosophy in the streets. A seventh-century Coptic bishop would later describe her as "devoted at all times to magic, astrolabes and instruments of music" who "beguiled many people through [her] Satanic wiles," which sounds like a compliment to me.

SOPHIA BRAHE

CA. 1556–1643 You may have heard of Tycho Brahe, the famous Danish astronomer credited with, among many other discoveries, realizing that what we see in the night sky is not static but, in fact, constantly changing. Good ol' Tycho had a sister—Sophia—who assisted him with much of his research and about whom we almost never hear. (*Shocking*, I know.) Highly educated in horticulture, chemistry, medicine, literature, poetry, and alchemy, Sophia not only taught herself astronomy but also paid for books and translations with her own money, like a true independent woman. As a teenager,

Sophia helped her brother lay the groundwork for planetary orbit prediction, including predicting a lunar eclipse. Though she's often denied credit where credit is due, Pierre Gassendi's seventeenth-century biography of Tycho does give her a little shout-out, saying that Sophia "love[d] astronomy" and was "especially ready to engage in these exciting studies."

ÉMILIE DU CHÂTELET

1706–1749 Gabrielle Émilie Le Tonnelier de Breteuil, marquise du Châtelet (heck of a name!), lived in France during the so-called Age of Enlightenment, when humanity was emerging from the (metaphorical) darkness of times past and learning all the things. A prodigy who, as a teenager, used math to win at gambling in order to bankroll her book habit, Émilie went *hard* after her education, hiring private tutors and attending lectures dressed as a man (since they were all *no girls allowed* about it). She also lived and collaborated with the writer and philosopher Voltaire for many years. She published many influential papers, including criticisms of John Locke (not the *LOST* guy, the Enlightenment philosopher). Émilie's scholarship even predicted the existence of infrared light—a pretty solid foundation for her arguments that women *too* deserved higher education.

MARIE CURIE

1867–1934 No chapter on women in science is complete without the great Marie Curie. After moving from Poland to Paris at age twenty-four, Marie studied during the day and tutored in the evenings to make rent (for an unheated attic) before obtaining two master's degrees from the Sorbonne: one in physics and one in math. After years of rebuffing advances from her fellow scientist Pierre Curie, Marie married him in 1895 and stayed to do doctoral work at the Sorbonne. Not only was Marie the university's first female professor, she also developed the theory of radioactivity for her dissertation (not bad). She went on to discover two elements (radium and polonium); prove that atoms are divisible; found the Curie Institute; win Nobel Prizes (the first woman ever to win and, remarkably, the only woman ever to win *two*); and coin the term *radioactivity*. Sadly, all this excellence had some unfortunate side effects (like basically melting to death from the inside because of radiation poisoning), but it was all in the name of science, and that's about as metal as it gets.

LANYING LIN

1918–2003 Lanying Lin, the "Mother of Aerospace Materials" and the "Mother of Semiconductor Materials," was born into a prestigious Chinese family and spent her entire life battling to pursue her passion for science. Lanying was accepted to China's Fukien Christian University to study physics at age eighteen and continued her studies at thirty, after having taught for several years at her alma mater. After moving to the United States and obtaining a PhD in solid state physics from the University of Pennsylvania, she worked as a semiconductor engineer before returning to her homeland (though the FBI tried to convince her to stay—that's how awesome her work was). Back in China, she developed the first silicon monocrystal and helped her country become a leader in microelectronics. In later years, Lanying began studying microgravity semiconductor materials (aka crystals in space) and teamed up with the All-China Women's Federation to fight for women's right to be educated.

ROSALIND FRANKLIN

1920–1958 Born to a prominent Jewish family in Notting Hill, London, Rosalind Franklin studied at Cambridge University and earned her PhD by age twenty-five, thanks in part to her work to help the war effort at the British Coal Utilisation Research Association. A few years later, she began work at King's College in London (which was co-ed, even though men and women were required to eat separately), where she did research using X-ray diffraction, a method of identifying the structure of molecules that she applied to DNA fibers. By January 1953, she'd concluded that DNA takes the double-helix form that we're now all so familiar with. Rightly realizing she was on to something, she sent her findings to the journal *Acta Crystallographica* in March—a full day before James Watson and Francis Crick, the so-called discoverers of the double helix, completed their model of the structure. Coincidence? Hardly. Watson and Crick's model was based on a photo of the double helix that *Rosalind* had taken, which they got their hands on through back channels. Watson—who told Rosalind to her face that he didn't think she was smart enough to interpret her own photos correctly—and Crick were awarded a Nobel prize for their work in 1962; Rosalind never was.

MARIE M. DALY

1921–2003 The first Black American woman to receive a doctorate in chemistry, Marie was the daughter of an immigrant from the British West Indies. She loved nothing more than to read about scientists from books in her grandfather's impressive library. Her father had run low on funds before he could finish his chemistry degree, but Marie was determined to pick up where he left off. Busting through gender and race boundaries, she attended Queens College for her bachelor's degree in chemistry (with top honors!), NYU for her master's (in one year!), and Columbia for her doctorate. (Her professor at Columbia, the wheelchair-using biochemist and teacher Dr. Mary L. Caldwell, was also super rad.) Marie then went on to work at Howard University, the Rockefeller Institute, Columbia University, Yeshiva University, the American Heart Association, the Einstein College of Medicine, and the New York Academy of Sciences (*phew!*). She set up a scholarship in her father's name for Black science students at Queens College, forever cementing her dedication to education.

Q&A WITH
LYNN CONWAY,

COMPUTER SCIENTIST, ELECTRICAL
ENGINEER, AND SCIENCE EDUCATOR

Q: *When did you realize you were interested in science? Did anyone encourage you?*

My father was a chemical engineer and my mother a kindergarten teacher. Raised as a boy back in the 1940s/50s, I became fascinated with astronomy and electronics and enjoyed creating things. Although very shy, I did well in math and science. I had no concept of what it meant to have a career, but it somehow seemed predestined that I'd do science and engineering when I grew up. Some of my best teachers really reinforced that feeling.

Q: *Despite your pioneering work at IBM in the 1960s, you were fired for expressing your gender identity. Can you describe the difficulties and barriers to entry you experienced and how you overcame them?*

My gender struggles during childhood had a valuable side effect: my intellectual life became my escape. Later, at Columbia University, my capabilities came to the attention of IBM Research and I was asked to join the staff in 1964. I made pioneering computer research contributions at IBM and really loved the work there. Sadly, IBM fired me in 1968 when I revealed that I was transitioning.

Starting all over again in a secret new identity, I was very lucky to get a job as a contract programmer. Most men back then felt uncomfortable using computer keyboards, because they looked like "women's typewriters," so young women who'd been studying math and science had a chance to become much-needed programmers.

Because of all the research knowledge I gained in my secret past, I often surprised employers with what I could do, and I soon advanced to becoming a computer architect at Memorex Corporation. However, for many decades I lived in fear of being "outed" and again losing my career.

Q: *Your work in microelectronic chip design has had a major worldwide impact. What specifically did you do?*

Recruited by Xerox Palo Alto Research Center [PARC] in 1973, I invented some elegantly simplified methods that enabled computer engineers to design complex microelectronic chips, and I was principal author of the textbook *Introduction to VLSI Systems*. I then pioneered the teaching of these new methods while at MIT. My new VLSI [very-large-scale integration] course spread rapidly to over 100 universities worldwide and launched a revolution in VLSI microchip design during the 1980s. Back at PARC I also invented and demonstrated an Internet-based e-commerce system for rapid chip prototyping, thus spawning the "fabless-design + silicon-foundry" industrial paradigm of modern semiconductor-chip design and manufacturing.

But since as a woman I didn't "look like an engineer" during the 1970s, Silicon Valley's elites had no clue what I'd actually done back then, and almost all credit went to others. That began to change in 2012, when my "VLSI Reminiscences" were published in a special issue of the *IEEE Solid-State Circuits Magazine*, revealing how—closeted and hidden behind the scenes—I had conceived the ideas that reshaped an entire industry.

Q: *Part of your work illuminating and educating people on gender identity and gender transition involves a kind of gonzo journalism wherein you are exposed to hundreds of people's* *stories. What stands out to you most, or has had the biggest effect on you, during this process?*

When I retired from teaching at the University of Michigan in 1999, I began quietly "uncovering" my secret past on my website. Within a few years, the site became a beacon of hope and encouragement for trans people around the world.

I was stunned by the sheer numbers of people who began contacting me by email, especially the unexpectedly large numbers and great diversity of trans women. Until then, psychiatrists claimed that only 1 in 30,000 boys and 1 in 100,000 girls felt a strong need to correct their gender assignments. However, by doing some common-sense data gathering and using simple statistics, I determined that the number was no smaller than about 1 in 500—about 100 times more trans people than the psychiatrists thought there were! This also brought into doubt all their other "scientific" claims about trans people, many of which have since been refuted.

Q: *How have you seen the landscape improve for trans women in technology (partially due to your tireless effort)?*

In the last ten years or so, there have been remarkable shifts in the visibility and social acceptance of all LGBT people. There are now wonderful employment opportunities for trans women educated in science, technology, engineering, and math. Especially if they transitioned while in college or earlier and can begin their careers in their new identities.

However, the overall picture is still a mixed bag. Many social and emotional crosscurrents need to be navigated if someone transitions on the job. Highly capable minority trans women have enormous difficulties accessing a welcoming and supportive higher education. Truly helpful advice, counseling, and mentoring are often hard to come by. We also face ongoing difficulties with institutionalized transphobia in social sectors, such as policing and medicine.

Q: *What advice would you give young women (especially young trans women) who want to get into STEM?*

During this time of rapid cultural evolution, ever more people will participate in the adventure of expanding the techno-social envelope of "what it's possible to do." At the forefront of the Social Age will be those who creatively surf at the edge of science, technology, engineering, mathematics, architecture, design, and art. Being natural collaborators, women will be greatly advantaged because they easily gravitate into supportive self-empowerment groups where they can learn and share new ideas and methods. There's no better time than now for young women to get into STEM and get out there surfing on the wondrous incoming wave!

A pioneer in both the field of microelectronics chip design and activism for transgender women in STEM careers, **LYNN CONWAY** is professor emerita of electrical engineering and computer science at the University of Michigan in Ann Arbor. When not working, she enjoys going on outdoor adventures with her husband, Charlie. Learn more at lynnconway.com.

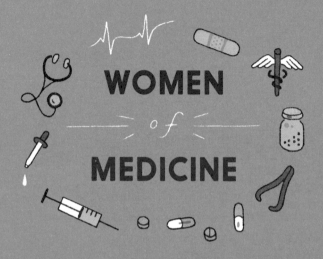

CHAPTER TWO

WOMEN

of

MEDICINE

You've probably been taught that women have "healing hands" and are "natural nurturers," but the fact is that some women are just naturally good at doctoring—not because of any sexist generalization, but because they are smart as all get-out and work hard for their patients. Throughout the history of medicine, ladies have consistently preferred being treated by other ladies, be it because of body shame (a whole 'nother issue entirely), fear, discomfort, or just a desire to feel that the person talking to you about your problems can truly understand what you're going through. Sadly, for most of time, getting a lady doctor was impossible; strict laws forbade women from practicing medicine, mostly because men were afraid they'd be too good at it (and they were). But a few incredible pioneers bucked the system to fight for their patients, and their courage and accomplishments deserve to be known.

Jacqueline Felice
DE ALMANIA

active
ca.1322

ITALIAN PHYSICIAN

"I shall heal you, God willing,
if you have faith in me."

If you like women who take a serious stand for what's right, you will love Jacqueline Felice de Almania. Back in the fourteenth century (aka the late Middle Ages, a time when everyone had weirdly flat faces, if you believe the artwork), Paris flourished as a center of learning . . . as long as you were a Christian man. For Jewish women like Jacqueline (or Jacoba, the Latinized form of her name), education was hard to come by, and practical work like doctoring was forbidden. But that didn't stop our gal from standing up for herself, even in court.

We don't know much about Jacqueline's early life, but from the Austrian preacher and scholar Father Heinrich Denifle's four-volume *Cartulary of the University of Paris* (an 1889 transcription of documents concerning the university in the Middle Ages), we do know that she was a Jewish gal born in Florence sometime in the 1290s. Given the fancy honorary title *domina* in the writings of others (and given the extra-fancy title *nobilis mulier domina Jacoba*, or "noble woman and mistress," in her own words), we also know that she was, indeed, fancy: an upper-class lady who, by the 1320s, had picked up an impressive knowledge of medicine and made her way to Paris. There she became one of only a few female physicians (technically called empirics, because they weren't allowed to be called doctors) then practicing in Paris. How few? Well, in 1292 they numbered only eight. Not exactly a woman-dominated industry.

Despite being rare, these women doctors provided essential care. Empirics were known mostly for assisting with reproductive health (think midwifery). But plenty of upper-class women (like Jacqueline) learned a wide spectrum of medical skills, making them the kind of all-purpose doctor that today we'd call a general practitioner. Unfortunately for Jacqueline and her patients, having successful women doctors was *not* something that governments historically wanted or allowed. Not when there was regulating to do—and *definitely* not when there was money to be made. The dudes in power needed some kind of strategy to prevent anyone who wasn't a rich white Christian guy from treating patients, especially the kind of rich, upper-class patients who could pay hecka cash.

And so in 1271 the medical facility of the University of Paris invoked an obscure 200-year-old statute that made it illegal for anyone to practice medicine without a specially obtained church license. Naturally, this license could be obtained only by completing courses at the university—courses that women and Jewish people weren't allowed to take. Even worse, the required courses weren't the type of hands-on, practical, head-bone-connected-to-neck-bone stuff a doctor should probably know; instead, they were theoretical and philosophical classes that focused on the writings of Aristotle, Hippocrates, Plato, and Galen, a Roman "doctor" who was all about examining men's "temperaments." This meant that the licensed doctors in Paris were not terribly effective (unless the effect you wanted was a doctor who slaps leeches on your body and leaves you to die while shrugging a lot and citing Hippocrates). These trained "physicians" looked down on surgeons and apothecaries—the doctors who, although not licensed, could in fact *save your life* by cutting horrible stuff out of you or prescribing medicine. Worst of all: anyone found practicing without a license (and actually saving lives) could be reported and shut down by no less than the pope for, as the law put it, endangering the public by a *lack of knowledge.*

Jacqueline wasn't about to let a silly thing like near-universal condemnation keep her from healing people (she ain't afraid of no pope!), and she continued to treat patients as she always had. Not surprisingly, her persistence did *not* go over so well with the old boys' medicine club, especially since—as a well-educated, upper-class woman—Jacqueline was "stealing" away their wealthier patients. (Because, you know, the most important part of medical care is making money.) So on August 11, 1322, a group of physicians dragged Jacqueline to court on the charge of illegal doctoring—or, as the official court documents stated, because she "visited many sick people suffering from serious illness . . . examining their urine both jointly and separately, taking their pulse, and feeling, palpating and holding their bodies and limbs." In addition, she made "an agreement with them to cure them" and distributed "syrups to drink, pain relievers, laxatives and digestives, both liquid and nonliquid, as well as aromatic, and other potions." (Which sounds an awful lot like *exactly what a doctor is supposed to do.* How dare she!)

Luckily, Jacqueline had top-notch legal counsel. Her attorney brought some of her recovered patients to the stand, including Joana Bilbaut, whose "feverish illness," despite the attention of "very many physicians," had made her so sick that "she could not speak, and the aforesaid physicians consigned her to death." Along came Dr. Jacqueline with her pulse-palpating and her syrup-giving and *ta-da,* Joana was good as new. In fact, nearly all of the eight patients who testified said that they had been told by the city's licensed physicians that they were as good as dead. Jacqueline's attorney made sure to tell the court that she had "successfully cared for many sick people whom master physicians had failed to cure." Not only that, she also refused payment!

Jacqueline spoke up for herself, too. She argued that the centuries-old law being levied against her was to prevent "idiots and fatuous ignorant" people from practicing medicine—and therefore this fatuous and ignorant law should not apply to her. She went on: "It is better and more suitable and proper that a woman wise and experienced in the art should visit sick women," for "it used to be that a woman allowed herself to die, rather than reveal her secret illnesses to a man . . . because of the shame which she would have suffered in revealing them." (Of course, we know that Jacqueline treated both men and women, so this was just a clever defense tactic.)

Unfortunately, "saying things that matter" tends not to persuade bigots with power; the judge dismissed her claims and those of the witnesses, saying that Jacqueline's testimony "ought not to stand and is frivolous since it is certain that a man approved in the aforesaid art could cure the sick better than any woman." (Right—*certain*, even though the cured patients were standing! Right! There!) In a sad end to this tale, Jacqueline and three other empirics were banned from practicing medicine, threatened with excommunication, and fined sixty livres. Even more sadly, Jacqueline's verdict discouraged women from practicing medicine in France for the next five and a half centuries. (If there's any justice in the world, the judge died from a totally curable illness while covered in leeches.) Still, you have to admire Jacqueline for not only being amazing at her job but also knowing her worth *and* sticking up for it, even when her livelihood was on the line.

We don't know what became of Jacqueline after her trial, but I'd like to imagine that she spent her days in a nice warm country healing ladies 'til she dropped. And that, from the afterlife, she forces the judge who condemned her to watch every graduation ceremony of women medical students ever.

Elizabeth and Emily
BLACKWELL

1821–
1910

1826–
1910

AMERICAN DOCTORS
AND HOSPITAL FOUNDERS

"The practice of medicine by women is a growing influence, and cannot be overlooked."

A ny lady in America who has graduated from medical school has done so thanks to these two amazing sisters. (Not *literally.* They do not show up from beyond the grave and do all your homework for you, but they paved the way for your diploma nonetheless.) Elizabeth and Emily Blackwell made it possible for all our lady selves to get into medical school if we so choose—and considering that women make up about half of all med school students these days, that's 100 percent a big deal.

The Blackwell sisters were born in Bristol, England, in the 1820s to a large (as in, seven siblings and four aunts) social-justice-minded family. Their father, Samuel, was a sugar refiner, and the family moved in accordance with his business, first to New York City in 1830 and then to Ohio a decade later. In Ohio, Samuel tried to set up a sugar factory using locally sourced ingredients like sugar beets so that he could stop relying on the slave trade for his income (which was a bold move, considering that almost everything relied on enslaved labor back then). Unfortunately, the factory failed and Samuel Blackwell died shortly thereafter. But his legacy lived on, both in the "deeply ingrained sense of civil duty" sense and in the "beet-load of debt" sense. To make ends meet, Elizabeth began traveling across the United States as a teacher. During these trips she met a woman dying of uterine cancer who mentioned that her treatment would have been much more pleasant had she had a woman doctor.

For Elizabeth, that was all it took to rev up the ol' "helping the less fortunate" Blackwell spirit. After saving the necessary $3,000 for medical school, Elizabeth started querying universities about admission. The replies were negative in all senses of the word. Most schools refused her request; one suggested that she just pretend to be a man, while another replied "that it was an utter impossibility for a woman to obtain a medical education; that the idea though good in itself, was eccentric and utopian, utterly impracticable!" Apparently, the medical school faculties were equal parts afraid that she, as a woman, would be far too stupid to be a doctor or that she, as a woman, would be far too *good* as a doctor, running all the men out of their jobs. Ultimately, Elizabeth received a conditional offer from Geneva Medical College (now Hobart) in upstate New York. The school agreed to put her admission to a vote, and if even *one* of her 150 male classmates said no, she would not be admitted. Luckily, they all thought it was a hilarious joke being played by a rival college (seriously!), and every one of them voted yes. All joking stopped shortly thereafter when Elizabeth marched in to class.

The town wasn't quite sure what to make of her. "When I entered college in 1847," said Elizabeth seventeen years later, at an address on the medical education of women, "the ladies of the town pronounced the undertaking crazy, or worse, and declared they would die rather than employ a woman as a physician. . . . I had so shocked Geneva propriety that the theory was fully established either that I was a bad woman, whose designs would gradually become evident, or that, being insane, an outbreak of insanity would soon be apparent." Quite a few news articles appeared on her acceptance and class attendance, although Elizabeth brushed them off, being "much annoyed by such public notices." She had bigger things to focus on, like *actual medical work*.

Determined to prove her equal worth, Elizabeth wrote a letter to her professor insisting she was capable of attending dissections. It worked—not only was she allowed to participate, but her prof read the letter to the class. (In her diary, however, Elizabeth admitted that all that dead body stuff was a little, well, *affecting*: "My delicacy was certainly shocked, and yet the exhibition was in some sense ludicrous. I had to pinch my hand till the blood nearly came, and call on Christ to help me from smiling, for that would have ruined everything; but I sat in grave indifference, though the effort made my heart palpitate most painfully.") Her persistence paid off, and on January 23, 1849, Elizabeth became the first woman in America to earn a medical degree. Called last to the stage, she was the only graduate for whom the president stood and bowed.

Unfortunately, not everyone thought she was righteously awesome. The school's dean, Dr. Charles Lee, wrote only a few years later that the "inconvenience" of female medical students was so great that he would "feel compelled on all future occasions to oppose such a practice." The *Boston Medical and Surgical Journal* seemed to agree, calling Elizabeth's degree "a farce" and hoping, "for the honor of humanity," that she would be the last woman MD in America. (Yeesh!) Luckily for us all, the great British satire and humor magazine *Punch!* knew what was up, and in 1849 its editors published a lovely poem called "An M. D. in a Gown":

> *Young ladies all, of every clime,*
> *Especially of Britain,*
> *Who wholly occupy your time*
> *In novels or in knitting,*
> *Whose highest skill is but to play,*
> *Sing, dance, or French to clack well,*
> *Reflect on the example, pray*
> *Of excellent Miss Blackwell!*

Clearly, Emily Blackwell was listening. The younger Blackwell sister had grown into a tall, shy, ginger-haired woman who longed for "life instead of stagnation." Much as she loved studying birds and plants at home, she wanted to follow in her older sister's footsteps and get herself to med school. Emily's path would be just as hard as Elizabeth's, if not more so. She was rejected by eleven medical schools because of her gender, and when she was finally accepted into Chicago's Rush Medical College, the school demanded she leave a year later after her (whiny) (male) classmates complained to the Medical Society of Illinois. But Emily was undeterred. She studied privately, visiting as many clinical lectures as she could, until at last she was accepted at Western Reserve University's medical school in Cleveland, thanks to the forward thinking of one Dean John Delamater and the support of the Ohio Female Medical Education Society. She earned her medical degree in 1854 and, after bopping around Europe for a bit, headed back to New York City.

At last, the sisters were primed to combine their powers. In 1857 Elizabeth, who had lost both an eye and her hopes of becoming a surgeon during a stint working in Europe, teamed up with Emily and a German doctor named Marie Zakrzewska to establish the New York Infirmary for Indigent Women and Children. The hospital occupied a sixteen-room house and employed a full female staff of physicians, executives, and trustees. Emily was in charge of operations and succeeded in securing long-term state support—$1,000 a year and official recognition—by heading to Albany with one of the trustees to demand it in person. (Not bad for a shy girl!) Yet somehow Dean Emily still managed to find time to help train nurses during the Civil War. At the time, the medical college had one of the best programs in the country: a full four-year comprehensive, complete with incredible lab space, amazing clinical training, and a policy of No Boyz Allowed. By 1876 the facility had expanded to include another mansion and capacity for over 7,500 in- and outpatients per year. By the turn of the twentieth century, they'd trained almost four hundred lady doctors.

Of course, not everything went smoothly. Elizabeth occasionally butted heads with Emily (sisters, you know how it goes) and moved to London, where she got a little, um, out there with her ideas about how germs aren't real and vaccines are bad and we all get sick because of moral corruption. She never married, claiming that "I cannot find my other half here, but only about a sixth, which would not do" (even though she'd received what was basically a proposal from none other than Florence Nightingale, who said Elizabeth would "want no other husband" but her if they ended up together). Instead, Elizabeth created her own family by adopting an Irish girl (who ended up working more as Elizabeth's servant, unfortunately).

Emily stuck things out in New York, and while training at the clinic she met the love of her life, Dr. Elizabeth Cushier. They moved in together in 1882 (just gals bein' pals, right, history?), along with their adopted daughter Nanni. Emily found Cushier to be hugely valuable to both the infirmary and the college after her sister's departure ("What I should have done without her help in the work the last few years I do not know"). But when Cornell University started admitting women in 1899, the two of them decided to shut down the school in the interest of promoting nongendered education. Emily became a member of the New York County Medical Society in 1871 (after years of turning down the honor because of her shyness), and she even served on a committee that raised $50,000 for Harvard—on the catch that the university start accepting women to its medical school. Officials turned the money down.

In their retirement, Emily and Cushier traveled together for eighteen months. Cushier was only sixty-two years old, and though she "did not feel that [she] actually needed to make the break at this time, [she] could not resist the thought of travel with such a companion." (Too sweet.) Emily died in Maine in 1910, just a few months after the death of Elizabeth. Today their legacy lives on, and it's great to think how super-psyched they'd be to see so many American women becoming doctors. So let's double ghost fist-bump these sisters right now. Do it. Do it. No one's watching. Do it.

Ogino
GINKO

1851–
1913

JAPANESE DOCTOR,
HOSPITAL FOUNDER,
AND WRITER

"Anything is possible if done with conviction. I was the only one who could achieve my ambitions."

If you just started thinking, "Hm, this is cool and all, but where are all the radical Japanese ladies?" please join me as we revisit one so spectacular that it's startling we haven't all heard of her bravery, brains, and brilliant work: Ogino Ginko, the woman who opened the door to medical school for women in Japan.

Ginko was born to the Ogino family in 1851, just two years before the start of the Meiji Restoration (aka a time when white folks showed up and started ordering Japanese people around, a move you may be familiar with from similar historical story lines all over the world for all of time). After Commodore Matthew Perry of the U.S. Navy "opened" Japan to the West in 1853 (could he *be* any more entitled?), the country was saddled with some seriously unfair trade treaties and a sudden urge to Westernize to compete in the world market. By the 1870s, national projects like *fukoku kyōhei* (rich country, strong army) and *bunmei kaika* (civilization and enlightenment) saw fiefs supplanted by official prefectures and feudal samurai lords ousted by new government, class, and legal systems. Modernization swept through railways, communications, banks, factories, and mines, as well as the institution of compulsory education for all children—to a point. Middle schools and universities remained men-only zones; so if you were a woman, postprimary education was not happening unless you wanted to become a teacher or a midwife. There just wasn't much that women were allowed to do. Take it from the Japanese officials who, on a trip to the United States, came face-to-face with the pants-wearing Civil War physician Dr. Mary Walker and wrote how they couldn't wait to get back to their own country, where "the woman rules within [the home] but she has no role outside it."

Ginko was the fifth daughter of the village headman in the town that is currently Kumagaya (about an hour north of Tokyo). At age sixteen she made what her family considered a good match and married the son of a wealthy director of Ashikaga Bank. Tragically, marriage was not so great for Ginko—her husband was less of a "good match" and more of a jerk who eventually gave her gonorrhea. In 1870s Japan, there weren't a whole lot of grounds on which women could divorce their husbands, but thankfully "my creep husband gave me an STD" was one of them, and three years later Ginko was able to free herself. The disease was treatable, but that didn't make the healing process any easier. On top of the terrible shame of her husband's infidelity, Ginko endured almost two years of medical visits, during which a doctor examined her delicate parts, before fully recovering. Infuriated and mortified by the whole episode ("being examined by a male doctor was always a misery," she said), Ginko dreamed of a country where women would never have to endure the same pain. Humiliation at the hands of doctors wasn't an issue only for women with STDs, either; pregnant women in Japan would almost never get check-ups out of embarrassment about their bodies. Feeling so "acutely" that Japan needed lady physicians, she decided to become one.

For her formative education, Ginko had attended Tokyo Women's Normal School (today's Ochanomizu University). Now she had to worry about getting into a medical program, which at the time were universally *bro*grams. With the help of Ishiguro Tadanori, president of the Red Cross Society, and the feminist activist Shimoda Utako (who would later found two schools for women), Ginko was able to sit in on classes at the Kōjuin, a private school at Kōju Hospital. Taking classes at the Kōjuin was challenging, and not just because of the coursework. The other students acted deplorably toward Ginko, and the entire institutional structure didn't care one iota about helping her. Because Ginko was tough as nails, she endured the abuse from students and teachers alike, and she did it while supporting herself financially (because her family was really not down with the whole "I'm going to be a doctor now" situation).

Her endurance paid off, and Ginko graduated from the Kōjuin in 1882. Happy ending, right? Not so fast: as part of the new laws established by the Meiji government to better regulate national health standards, one could become a licensed medical practitioner only by passing two state examinations—exams that women, of course, weren't permitted to take. Ginko requested that the government allow women to sit for the exam, writing a very kind letter, which one can only imagine officials cackled over before slowly ripping it to pieces. Sensing she would have to go hard or go home, Ginko dug up historical precedent from the *Ryō no gige*, an eighth-century legal commentary, and marched directly into the office of Nagayo Sensai, director of the national hygiene bureau. The official was so impressed with her evidence and determination, he decided that, from 1884 on, women would be allowed to take the National Physician Licensing Examination. Of the three women who sat for the tests that year, Ginko was the only one who passed.

Once licensed, Ginko wasted no time. She opened the Ogino Hospital in Yushima to create a specialized space for obstetrician/gynecologists and managed to land a plum gig as a staff doctor at Meiji Gakuin Women's University. After marrying a Protestant priest in 1890, Ginko and her second husband headed north to Hokkaidō, where she set up a practice and helped countless women in need. On top of all that, Ginko was also part of the newly formed Tokyo Women's Reform Society, also called the Tokyo Women's Christian Temperance Union. But where similar organizations around the world were concerned primarily with stopping people from drinking too much, the Tokyo society had other goals. They wanted the Meiji Restoration to expand and modernize opportunities for *all* Japanese people. In particular, the society opposed such oppressive traditions as women remaining silent in front of men, killing themselves to protect their virginity, selling their bodies to help their parents earn money, and changing their appearance after marriage (by blackening their teeth and shaving their eyebrows, in accordance with the beauty standards of the time). Thankfully for us in the future, Ginko wrote at length about her experience of becoming a doctor, as well as the overall advancement of women in Japan, in the journal *Jogaku Zasshi*, whose English title, *The Magazine of Women's Education* or *Ladies' Enlightenment*, sounds awesome no matter how you translate it.

In 1908, following her husband's death, Ginko moved back to Tokyo and continued to run Ogino Hospital until her death from hardened arteries in 1913. Today she is remembered as a feminist and a pioneer; she even has a minor planet named after her (10526), which, if we ever get around to starting that all-lady space colony, would be the perfect place to live happily and healthily ever after. But the best way to honor Ginko is to let her story teach you to find your strength. After all, as Ginko once said, "to learn from the past is the true nature of learning."

Anandibai
JOSHI

1865–
1887

INDIAN DOCTOR

"The voice of humanity is with me and I must not fail. My soul is moved to help the many who can not help themselves."

Sometimes a woman's life is so extraordinary, it's hard to believe that no one has made a movie about her. Case in point: is Anandi Joshi. Her extraordinary story has everything: adversity, triumph, women's health, and a strong female friendship that spanned oceans. But like every superhero deserving of a film franchise, Anandi started out as just an ordinary, curious kid.

Growing up in the once-prosperous coastal town of Kalyan, India, a young Yamuna (as she was known at birth) wanted more than anything to learn—a big dream at a time when women were denied even basic literacy. Fortunately, her father encouraged her passions and found her a teacher, a postal worker named Gopalrao, who began giving her lessons. Yamuna's family was part of a particularly high-class caste but had recently lost their fortune, so when Gopal was transferred to a new city, Yamuna was terrified that she would have to stop her lessons and start living the life of a typical Brahmin girl. "I thought that I should never learn any more," she later said, "and I would rather have died." To solve the problem of both her education and the financial burden on her family, Yamuna and Gopal married when Gopalrao was twenty-six years old and Yamuna was only nine.

Which we can all agree is pretty terrible. The ingrained social institution of child marriage prevented girls from attending school after they were wed and generally kept them powerless; the practice wouldn't be outlawed in India for another fifty-five years.

But from what we can tell, Gopal was—at least in one way—not completely bound to the cultural mores of his day. He gave his young wife the name by which she would be known for the rest of her life—Anandibai, meaning "joy of my heart"—and respected her desire to learn. Anandi's education continued after marriage and included lessons in English; she grew into relative independence and the belief that "no man or woman should depend upon another for maintenance and necessaries."

Sadly, tragedy wasn't far off. When Anandi was between twelve and fourteen years old, she bore a son who lived only ten days. Anandi was heartbroken, knowing that her baby might have stood a chance if she and Gopal had access to proper medical care. It was then that she decided to become a doctor. But doing so was easier said than done. When Anandi attempted to attend classes or go to hospitals in India, people were *rather* displeased (sorry, understatement: they would spit, throw rocks, and scream obscenities at her). On top of that abuse, she and her husband were living in an area where few people shared their Maharashtra Hindu customs, which included certain types of food, clothing, fasting days, and holidays. After moving north from Calcutta to Serampore and finding no new opportunities there, Anandi decided it was time to search farther afield—as in halfway around the world farther. So in 1880 Gopal wrote to the American missionary Royal Wilder to ask for Wilder's help, explaining that he wanted to move to the United States so that his wife could study medicine. Wilder declined in a response he published in Princeton University's *Missionary Review*. (Brief paraphrased summary: "Not unless you convert to Christianity!!!!! LOL.")

The exchange caught the attention of one Theodicia Carpenter of Roselle, New Jersey, who happened to have picked up a copy of the journal while waiting for a dental appointment. Believing that the truly Christian thing was to be nice to people (and that ladies needed to stick together), Theodicia started writing letters to Anandi; over the next few years, the two women exchanged newspapers, hair, magazines, pictures, and flowers (in other words, the movie version would totally pass the Bechdel test). Anandi called Theodicia her "Aunt," but also totally called out her privilege: "Your American widows may have difficulties and inconveniences to struggle with, but weighed in the scale against ours, all of them put together are but as a particle against a mountain." Theodicia, in turn, sent medicine when Anandi was ill and said that her door was always open. But as much as she longed to see her friend, Anandi just could not afford the trip—as a Brahmin woman, she wasn't even supposed to travel overseas.

Instead, Anandi took action. On February 24, 1883, with no notes or prepared remarks, she marched into the Serampore College Hall and gave a speech to the town—the first woman ever to do so. "There is a growing need for Hindu lady doctors in India," she stated, "and I volunteer to qualify myself for one." Unafraid even of excommunication, she declared that she would travel to the United States to learn and then return home to open a college for the instruction of women in medicine: "I do not fear it [excommunication] in the least. . . . I will go as a Hindu, and come back here to live as a Hindu." And then she dropped the proverbial mic and strutted outta there.

Her ploy totally worked. The director-general of the post office in India set up a fund for her education, and donations began pouring in from the governor general, lieutenant governor, chief justice, and more. Having raised enough for a single ship ticket, Anandi left her husband behind, with his blessing but, she wrote, "against the combined opposition of my friends & caste." She was on a mission to "render to my poor suffering country women the true medical aid they so sadly stand in need of, and which they would rather die for than accept at the hand of a male physician."

And so in June 1883, Anandi headed to New Jersey, finally meeting her "Aunt" Theodicia and becoming the first Hindu woman to set foot in America. Anandi, Theodicia, and other lady doctors had written in advance to Rachel Bodley, dean of the Woman's Medical College of Pennsylvania, to ask for admittance—which Anandi was granted, along with a scholarship to cover the remainder of her $325.50 degree and a place to live in the dean's own house. Anandi—whom Rachel would call a "brave little pioneer" with a "beautiful life"—flourished, finishing a four-year medical degree in just three. She graduated on March 11, 1886, with her husband in the crowd; her thesis, titled "Obstetrics among the Aryan Hindoos," was not only the longest of the year but also widely circulated. After Queen Victoria (!) read a copy sent by Dean Bodley, a royal secretary wrote to express thanks and "to assure you that the Queen has read the paper with much interest."

Sadly, Anandi's health had been steadily in decline since she had contracted tuberculosis while in Calcutta. After graduation, she was forced to decline a trip around America as well as an internship at the New England Hospital for Women and Children. Instead, she accepted a position at Albert Edward Hospital in Kolhapur, assuming the roles of physician-in-charge of the female ward and head of a new program to teach girls to be general practitioners. Despite her best efforts, her health took a turn for the worse when she headed back to India in October 1886; she died three months later in her mother's arms.

Despite her earlier fears of exclusion, upon her death Anandi was far from a pariah. Her obituary in India praised her for proving that "the great qualities—perseverance, unselfishness, undaunted courage and an eager desire to serve one's country—do exist in the so-called weaker sex." Anandi's ashes were sent to Theodicia, who buried them in her own family's cemetery in Poughkeepsie, which is just about as perfect a tearjerker ending as we could ask for. Get on it, Hollywood.

Marie EQUI

1872–1952

AMERICAN DOCTOR AND
BIRTH CONTROL ADVOCATE

*"I'm going to speak when and
where I wish. No man will stop me."*

I magine if Dr. Quinn, Medicine Woman, had been a hard-core birth control advocate and proud lesbian who didn't hesitate to beat up anyone who tried to wrong her. Sound awesome? Well, let me welcome you to the life and times of Marie Equi.

The fifth child of Italian and Irish immigrants who had faced no small share of hardship in their own lives, Marie was born in 1872 in New Bedford, Connecticut. At the time, the town was famous for its textile production, and young Marie got to know the industry up close and personal when she was forced into factory work as a child of eight years old. This being the pre-safety-inspection days, she (and a ton of other girls under sixteen years old) faced horrible working conditions, including twelve-hour days, lung problems caused by cotton-dust inhalation, and dangerous equipment that wrought horrible injuries and death—you know, good ole-timey factory fun. The work took such a toll on her health that Marie had to leave home and live with relatives, first in Florida, then in Italy, to recover from tuberculosis. She was only seventeen years old.

But Marie was tough as heck, and soon she got a clean bill of health. Upon returning to the United States, she reunited with her childhood friend Bessie Holcomb, who had taken advantage of the Homestead Act of 1862 to pick up a pretty piece of Oregon property.

Bessie now owned a sweet little farmhouse on over one hundred acres west of the city of The Dalles and, more important, far away from her family. According to the *Dalles Chronicle* in 1893, Bessie's family definitely did not approve of her, *ahem*, "singular infatuation" with Marie. The couple found themselves a house and lived in what might have been known, had Marie been more well-off, as a "Boston marriage" (a term used to describe two single women living together, sometimes platonically, sometimes not).

Marie would go on to do some lovely and charitable things with the rest of her life, but if someone tried to screw with her lady, the gloves came off. One particularly passionate run-in occurred around June 1893. Bessie, who was a teacher, was owed the last $100 of her promised salary from one Reverend Orson D. Taylor of the Wasco Independent Academy, and Marie wanted him to pay up. Though Bessie tried to convince Marie to threaten him gently with an umbrella, Marie had more convincing methods in mind. As the *Dalles Times-Mountaineer* reported, Marie "horsewhipped Taylor from his office to the Methodist church" to the cheers of onlookers. (The press also wrote that Marie was so stirred to justice because she was "very much attached to [Bessie], and her friendship amounts to adoration." Just gals bein' pals, surely!) As it turned out, Reverend Taylor was a universally hated "smooth speaking scoundrel" who had scammed the people of The Dalles out of their money in a bunch of garbage real-estate schemes. The town's businessmen were so grateful for Marie's vigilante justice that the very next day they bought her a new dress, since "the one she wore during the encounter [had] been destroyed." Townspeople also raffled off the horsewhip for much more than the owed $100, all of which went to Marie and Bessie; and when Marie was charged with assault and battery, they raised the $250 needed for her bond in under five minutes. Best of all, that same week the scumbag Reverend Taylor was arrested and accused of embezzling $50,000.

But a horsewhip isn't the most effective way to help the less fortunate, and so in 1897 Marie and Bessie moved to San Francisco so that Marie could study, first at the Physicians and Surgeons Medical College and then at the University of California Medical Department. Even though at that time only around 3 percent of doctors in America were women, Marie wanted more than anything to help patients who had suffered as she had when young. She finished her degree in Portland in 1903, making her one of the first sixty women to become a doctor in Oregon. (Without Bessie, alas, for by then they had gone their separate ways.)

Although she earned a commendation and a medal from both the U.S. Army and the governor of California for helping victims of the 1906 San Francisco earthquake, Dr. Marie made her chief focus women's reproductive health. She treated everyone without discrimination, even charging wealthy women more so that she could cover the costs of reproductive care for impoverished Portlandians. Providing birth control and abortions was still forbidden in the United States, but savvy Marie knew how to circumvent the laws. When a special deputy of the Multnomah County sheriff's office almost came to blows with her over the illegality of her practice, she reminded him that she had just performed an abortion for a young woman *he* had brought to her and that he "should be ashamed of himself" for his hypocrisy.

Happily, Marie would fall in love again. Two years after graduation, she met a medical assistant named Harriet Speckart, the wealthy niece of the man who founded the Olympia Brewing Factory. The attraction was decidedly mutual. The two women moved in together and did adorable things like place second in the Class A carriage and team competition at Portland's first official Rose Festival in 1917. Even when the relationship nearly cost Harriet her inheritance (notably when her staunchly homophobic family hired a private investigator to discredit her), the couple stuck fast and, after ten years together, adopted a little girl named Mary. Mary grew up calling Harriet "Ma" and Marie "Da" (since everyone else called her "Doc"); at the age of only sixteen, Mary would become the first woman in the Pacific Northwest to fly a plane solo. (Two-mom-parenting high-five!)

As the years passed, Marie supplemented her doctoring with political action, fighting for equal rights across class and gender boundaries, particularly women's suffrage (achieved in Oregon for female American citizens of all races in 1912, eight years before the Nineteenth Amendment to the U.S. Constitution!) and improved workers' rights. She often protested on behalf of local cannery workers at the Oregon Packing Company, where girls aged twelve to twenty were locked in a factory for more than twelve hours a day. When her patient Mrs. O'Connor, a pregnant Native American woman, was arrested for protesting, a furious Marie trailed two officers all the way to the police station, where she smacked them around and told the sheriff that he was, among other things, "a cowardly, atavistic creature," "a primitive puppy," and "a caveman." Mrs. O'Connor was released, and the *Oregonian* praised Marie for her "sulphuric eloquence." When in 1916 Marie and the noted birth control activist Margaret Sanger (with whom she might have been gal pals as well, judging by letters between them that describe kissing in "absolute surrender") were hauled off for helping to distribute a pamphlet on "family limitation," Marie stabbed her arresting officer with a pin, laughing while she told him that the weapon had been poisoned and he was about to "die a slow, lingering death." (He didn't die, but he did have his wound cauterized with acid—just in case.)

After that episode, Marie grew increasingly radicalized. When she protested the United States' involvement in World War I (thinking the conflict was nothing more than a capitalist cash grab), she was arrested under the Espionage Act and thrown into San Quentin

Prison. U.S. president Woodrow Wilson commuted her sentence, but she nevertheless spent ten months behind bars, during which time she often attended to the other thirty-one female inmates.

While Marie was imprisoned, Harriet and Mary moved to the seaside, separating from "Da" but remaining close for the rest of their lives. Upon her release for good behavior in August 1921, Marie began a relationship with another radical activist, Elizabeth Gurley Flynn, leader of the Industrial Workers of the World. Flynn called Marie "one of the most feared and hated women in the Northwest" (which means you know she did something right), and the two would take care of each other into their old age—a tender ending for one tough lady.

Other Amazing Women of Medicine

AGNODICE

4TH CENTURY BCE Although there's a chance that Agnodice's legendary life is more faux than fact, her story is still inspirational. Back in ancient Athens, common occurrences like childbirth, as well as preventable and treatable illnesses, could end up being fatal—largely because women had been banned, on penalty of death, from practicing medicine, and many ill or pregnant women patients refused to see male doctors. According to legend, Agnodice high-tailed it to Alexandria, where she studied all the medicine she could. She then returned to Athens disguised as a dude, intending to give women quality treatment that didn't make them uncomfortable. The city's doctors grew suspicious of how much their wives liked the new Mr. MD, and so they dragged Agnodice to court on charges of adultery and seduction. Unflappable Agnodice simply lifted her dress, flashing the courtroom her bits, and thereby (in the eyes of ancient Athens, anyway) proving her innocence. After which she was unstoppable, mostly because all the women in Athens threatened to *leave* if their favorite doctor was banned from treating them.

MARIA DALLE DONNE

1778–1842 Born to a poor peasant family of day laborers outside Bologna, Italy, Maria Dalle Donne and her supersmarts were recognized early on by a physician named Luigi Rodati (who may have been her uncle). Rodati brought her to the city center and had her educated in Latin, physics, philosophy, pathology, anatomy, obstetrics, and more; he then encouraged her to apply to the University of Bologna on a yearly scholarship. Having learned all the things, Maria graduated in 1799 with degrees in philosophy and medicine, making her the first female MD *ever*. Denied a teaching position for the usual reasons (oh, *womanhood*), she instead was given a laboratory and funding to continue her research—which was great while it lasted. Ever nimble, Maria then moved on to directing the university's school for midwives (which she ran out of her own home), training countless midwives to abandon the era's more barbaric practices in favor of safer, more hygienic care. In 1829, the science institute Accademia Benedettina awarded her the title of "academic," which was both well deserved and a huge understatement, considering all that she'd done.

REBECCA LEE CRUMPLER

1831–1895 In the days when professional medical care for Black people in America was essentially nonexistent, Rebecca Lee Crumpler had to bust her butt to gain entry to the New England Female Medical College. She was accepted in 1860—following eight years of work as an untrained nurse—and her 1864 graduation made her the first Black woman in America to become a doctor of medicine. Rebecca went on to establish practices in Boston and Richmond, Virginia, intending to help freed slaves, poor women, and children of color. She persisted in caring for her patients despite intense racism (and sexism) from male colleagues, druggists, and the general public. At age fifty-two, Rebecca published *A Book of Medical Discourses*, the only nineteenth-century medical text written by a Black woman, filled with tips and tricks on the medical care of women.

OKAMI KEIKO

1859–1941 After graduating from the Yokohama Kyoritsu Girls'

School in 1878 and a brief stint teaching English, Okami Keiko and her art teacher husband headed to America. With financial assistance from the Women's Foreign Missionary Society of the Presbyterian Church (whose members called her studies abroad "akin to heroism"), Keiko was able to enroll at the Woman's Medical College of Pennsylvania, where in 1889 she became the first Japanese woman to earn a degree in medicine in the West (graduating alongside Susan La Flesche Picotte, the first Native American woman with a degree in medicine). Keiko actually knew our girl Anandi Joshi (page 67)—they appear together in a really awesome graduation photo, along with a Kurdish Jewish woman who went on to practice medicine in Cairo. After returning to Japan, Keiko worked at Jikei Hospital; opened her own clinic, women's hospital, and nursing school; and became vice principal of Shoei Girls' School in Tokyo.

SARA JOSEPHINE BAKER

1873–1945 After her father and brother died of typhoid, Sarah Josephine "Jo" Baker sought an education from the Blackwell sisters' medical college, where she earned her degree in 1898. She set up a medical practice in New York City, and became a medical inspector with the New York City Health Department. Because at the time everyone was super unhygienic—Jo noted that babies in America had a higher mortality rate than soldiers in World War I—she went door to door in the Hell's Kitchen neighborhood, teaching mothers how to care for their children in a clean way. To get babies off to the freshest start possible, she also developed a licensing system for local midwives (home births had a lower infection rate than hospital births, thanks to her!). She even caught the infamous disease-spreading Typhoid Mary—*twice* (probably because, like any good superhero, she wanted to avenge her father's death from typhoid). Jo fought hard for suffrage, became a representative for the U.S. Health Committee to the League of Nations, and shared a home with the Australian writer Ida Alexa Ross Wylie (just gals bein' pals!).

FE DEL MUNDO

1909–2011 Born in Manila, Fe del Mundo decided she wanted to become a doctor after watching four of her siblings die during child-hood. She went on to do *so* well in medical school at the University of the Philippines that at the age of twenty-four, she was offered a full scholarship to any school in America by the Philippine president him-self. She chose Harvard, where she ended up enrolled in its medical school completely by accident; it didn't admit women, but officials were unaware of Fe's lady status when they accepted her. Fortunately, she excelled at pediatrics, and because the Harvard department couldn't give a good reason for her *not* to be admitted, she became the first woman to graduate from Harvard Medical School. In 1941, after a residency at the University of Chicago, a research fellowship back at Harvard Medical School, and a master's degree in bacteriology from Boston University, Fe returned to her home country, where she spent the rest of her life helping poor, sick children as much as she could, even selling her home to fund a children's medical center.

GURUBAI KARMARKAR

D. 1932 Another alumna of our beloved Woman's College of Pennsylvania, Gurubai Karmarkar earned her diploma in 1892, six years after her countrywoman Anandi Joshi (page 67) graduated. In 1893 Gurubai and her husband, who had been studying at Hartford Theological Seminary, returned to Bombay, India, where she began working at the American Marathi Mission, a position she would hold for the next thirty years. Gurubai helped the poor and the wealthy equally, but she was especially known for her work with children who suffered from famine and the plague. And if that wasn't impressive enough, Gurubai also gave lectures on the state of women in India, speaking out against child marriage, and encouraged other women to leave the country on medical missions. When she retired, a wing in Bombay's community welfare center Lincoln House (now the Nagpada Neighborhood House) was named in her honor.

Q&A <u>WITH</u>
DR. BUDDHINI SAMARASINGHE

MOLECULAR BIOLOGIST, CANCER RESEARCHER,
AND FOUNDER OF STEM WOMEN

Q: *When did you become interested in science as a career? Did anyone encourage you?*

I realized quite early that I wanted to know everything I could about science. My mother is a scientist (her subject area is chemistry) and a lecturer at the University of Sri Jayawardenepura in Sri Lanka. My parents were very encouraging of my interest in science. I narrowed it down to molecular biology in my teens when I read *Jurassic Park* and was fascinated with the descriptions of genes and cloning techniques. I didn't care so much about the dinosaurs, but loved the idea of the "genetic blueprint" that underlies every living thing on this planet.

Q: *What were some difficulties or barriers to entry you experienced while getting into STEM, and how did you overcome them?*

I didn't experience any difficulties because once I was sure I wanted to study molecular biology, I focused on getting the grades I needed to get into university in the UK. The culture shock was a bit difficult to adjust to at first, because I grew up in Sri Lanka. I think that's something every international student faces, especially when from a minority ethnic background. Language wasn't a barrier for me because I grew up speaking English; so it was amusing when people assumed my English wasn't very good simply because I was the wrong skin color for it!

Q: *Describe your cancer research and molecular biology work.*

Following my undergrad degree, I earned a PhD in molecular parasitology, studying a parasite that infected sheep. But at a fundamental level, all organisms have DNA, and very similar genetic pathways, so the techniques I learned could be applied to studying any form of life. That's the beauty of molecular biology; DNA is DNA, whether it comes from a worm or a fruit fly or a human. I became interested in cancer because, during the final year of my undergraduate degree, my father was diagnosed with lung cancer, and I wanted to understand the disease. He passed away a year before my PhD graduation, so I switched from studying parasites to studying cancer for my postdoctoral research. Instead of fearing cancer because I didn't know much about it, I wanted to learn more about it so I could fear it less, if that makes sense.

Q: *You're passionate about making science accessible to the masses, and as a science communicator you write about STEM without the jargon. Do you think platforms like YouTube and Twitter make it easier to interest more people in science?*

I became involved in science communication during my postdoctoral research because I realized that molecular biology was a mystery to so many people. I started doing Google Hangouts, interviewing scientists about their work, and all the resulting videos are on YouTube. I also started writing about cancer mechanisms for *Scientific American*. Social media platforms definitely help with making science accessible to the public, helping scientists connect with one another. This experience helped me establish myself as a science communicator, allowing me to leave academia and, since November 2014, focus on science communications full-time. I now work for a cancer charity, "translating" science into English for fundraising teams. My writing reaches so many people and helps raise money toward cancer research, and it feels very meaningful to me because of that.

Q: *Can you tell us a bit about STEM Women and its goals?*

STEM Women is an organization I created back in 2011, around the same time I got into science communications. I was aware that the role models we always talk about are people like Marie Curie, a remote figure in a black-and-white photograph. I wanted more current examples of women scientists, and their experiences, so I started collecting stories. I then became aware of issues like sexism in academia, and in 2013 I partnered with two other women scientists and we set up our website, which we use to discuss these issues, feature role models, and generally advocate for women in STEM.

Q: *What advice would you give young women who want to get into STEM?*

STEM subjects are not easy, but they are absolutely fascinating and rewarding. It's a way of understanding the world and navigating through it. The skills you learn by doing a STEM course will stay with you for the rest of your life—skills like critical thinking, organization, planning . . . these are all so important and they are learned, not taught.

A molecular biologist currently working on cancer research, **DR. BUDDHINI SAMARASINGHE** is also a passionate science communicator whose mission is to describe science, minus the jargon. She is also the creator of STEM Women (stemwomen.net), a website that celebrates and supports the careers of women in science, technology, engineering, and mathematics. You can learn more about Buddhini by following her on Twitter @DrHalfPintBuddy or visiting her website, jargonwall.com.

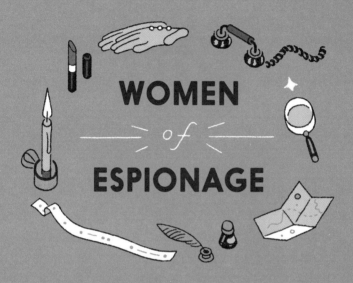

CHAPTER THREE

WOMEN

of

ESPIONAGE

Some women use their passion for extreme nerdery to delve deep into subjects like astrophysics and biochemistry—and that's amazing. But others are less about the theoretical and more about the going out into the world and working for serious immediate social change. These dames weren't cool with the establishment, and they realized their power to do good for their country. Using their unique skill sets (photographic memories, encrypting, forging, pretending to enjoy being in public with a bunch of people when they'd really rather be anywhere else) these incredible women shook things up like old-school *femmes Nikitas*. The time has come for their secret identities to be known.

Brita TOTT

active 1442–98

DANISH AND SWEDISH
SPY AND FORGER

Monarchies can be a pretty precarious form of government, which isn't so surprising if you stop to think about it. Give one person the ruling power of a deity and force them into diplomacy with other equally stubborn sovereigns—what could go wrong? Well, plenty. Especially when you have a spy like Brita Tott skulking around.

Brita Olufsdotter Tott (or Birgitte Olufsdatter Thott, depending on how Danish you are) had it good from the get-go—she was born rich. Her parents were the Danish knight and statesman Oluf Tott and the wealthy (as in huge tracts of land and massive castle in Vallø wealthy) heiress Karen Jensdotter Falk. In her youth, Brita's family was a political powerhouse in Scandinavia, even after her mother's death and father's remarriage; their machinations kept them well connected and in a position to influence policy in both Sweden and Denmark—a feat that, at the time, was extremely impressive. Why? Because by 1448 Denmark was ruled by King Christian, Sweden was ruled by King Charles, and Norway was in the rather unenviable position of having to choose to align with one neighboring nation or the other. All three countries had been united under Denmark's Queen Margaret I in 1397, but then her successor had un-united them. (A dude in power screwed something up? But that never happens!) After first choosing Charles of Sweden as an ally, the Norwegians flip-flopped and officially aligned with Christian of Denmark. Naturally, the Swedish were miffed (and probably made lots of anachronistic "Something is rotten" *Hamlet* jokes), and so fighting between Christian and Charles and their respective nations continued apace.

Despite being born to Danish parents, young Brita was on her way to becoming one of the Swedish king's BFFLs, thanks to her marriage in 1442 to the Swedish nobleman Erengisle Nilsson the Younger. A member of the elite Swedish Privy Council, Erengisle was a knight, judge, governor, and member of the aristocratic house known as Natt och Dag (aka Night and Day, aka the oldest living Swedish dynasty, aka Old Money). In case that wasn't impressive enough, his real house was a castle on a big ol' estate called Hammersta, in southeastern Sweden. Even though he had two children from his first (late) wife, Märta, Erengisle gave Hammersta (and all its farms and homes) to Brita as her *morgongåva*, the traditional "morning gift" a husband would bestow on his new wife the morning after their wedding. Which, in the case of preposterously rich people like Brita and Erengisle, was meant to provide security to the woman in case of her husband's death (a smart move in the 1440s, when you could drop dead from the Black Death, battle wounds, or not ever brushing your teeth).

Still, even as Brita started to rub shoulders with Sweden's King Charles (and her hubby began consulting on Super Important Kingly Business Decisions), one thing remained certain: Brita was Danish at heart, and she wasn't about to forget her roots. Yet instead of wearing her patriotism on her sleeve (or getting a cute Danish flag tattooed on her thigh), Brita decided to use her position of power and privilege to become a super-sneaky and viciously effective spy.

In 1451, when Sweden and Denmark stopped all their pretenses and flat out went to war, Brita realized she could be a huge help to her homeland—husband notwithstanding. She passed crucial information to the Danes about the strengths and weaknesses of Sweden's troops and its king so that her compatriots could stay one step ahead of the enemy. When Denmark invaded the bordering province of Västergötland, in southwestern Sweden, the soldiers crept right in and overtook the walled stronghold at Lödöse (present-day Gothenburg, now the country's second-largest city), with no one the wiser thanks to Brita's tips revealing the Swedish army's position. But Brita wasn't just sending messages far afield. At one point she was involved with a plot to assassinate King Charles, even though she hung out with him all the time and they were supposed to be *best buds.*

Unfortunately, the jig was soon up. Sir Tord Bonde, captain of Charles's forces, and his men rode all night through a storm to surprise the waiting Danes, retaking Lödöse. Inside the fortress he found, among other things, a bag full of letters from Brita to the Danish crown announcing all of Charles's plans. (Womp womp.) In 1452 Charles accused Brita of treason (or basically "being the worst friend ever"), a potentially fatal offense. In the tradition of all monarchies, however, the king's power was held in check by his nobles. Since the aristocracy knew that eliminating Brita would anger her powerful friends on both the Danish and the Swedish sides of her family, the sentence was commuted from being burned at the stake to being bricked into a wall to die a slow and agonizing death alone (which sounds *way* worse than the stake burning, no?). Ultimately, Brita's punishment was reduced to a mandatory lock-up in the Kalmar Nunnery (which sounds so *Sound of Music*). Erengisle lost his governorship, although he maintained his position on the council. (Times may change, but being rich is always a good way to stay in power.)

Once Brita finished her brief stint in nun prison, she decided to show she'd cleaned up her act by commissioning the artist Albertus

Pictor to travel to Ösmo church in Södermanland province, just ten minutes from Hammersta, and paint a series of murals. One of the paintings features Brita clad all in white, kneeling to ask for the Lord's forgiveness. So did this super-chill portrait mean she was ready for the straight-and-narrow path? Nope! Brita turned instead to forgery to increase her already huge fortune, creating fake wax seals, fancy stamps that acted as a kind of legally binding, easily reproduced signature. These allowed her to impersonate other people and move a bunch of money and property into her own holdings. Having ended up with so many seals, according to legend she directed a maid to throw a ton of them into the river outside the Hammersta estate (perhaps so that no one would be tempted to say, "Hey, wow, B, that's a lot of seals, considering you are one person and therefore should have only one seal. What is *up* with that?").

Brita may have engaged in some not-so-worthy endeavors, but she was likely trying to survive amid brutal medieval misogyny. For one thing, she was in danger of losing her home. After her husband's death in 1469, Brita claimed ownership of two properties: her mother's holdings in Vallø and Erengisle's holdings at Hammersta. The problem was that, a decade earlier, Brita had technically renounced her claim to Vallø so that her husband could hold on to Hammersta. Now that he was dead, Brita believed both lands were rightfully hers—Vallø because of inheritance, and Hammersta because of not only the morning-gift thing but also the three letters written by Erengisle stating unequivocally that it belonged to her. Nevertheless, people weren't accustomed to a single woman holding so much land, and they didn't buy her reasoning besides—especially not Brita's stepmother, who claimed Vallø for herself, nor Brita's stepchildren, who followed suit and claimed Hammersta. All this family infighting devolved into endless legal battles (and probably some super-awkward holidays). If only Brita could get her hands on official documentation that could override their claims . . .

Oh, wait—she could! Even though it was technically illegal, Brita did what she did best and forged documents stating that she was "equal to the best child" (in other words, just as worthy of the estate as her relatives), thereby restoring her rights to Vallø. With everything resolved, she promptly attempted to sell the property to the Danish crown for a ton of money. But by now the royals were wise to her tricks, and Brita was put on trial *again*, this time for forgery. Further complicating her predicament was the deathbed testimony of a guy claiming to be one of her forgers (it was later discovered that he was in fact working for a member of her evil stepfamily).

In 1479, for the second time in her life, Brita was found guilty—and once again she was let off without so much as a slap on the wrist. Sick of all the bickering and lawsuits, she eventually headed back to Denmark, where in 1484 she was made administrator of the royal lands of Dronningeholm, far north of Copenhagen. She went on to act as *länsman och godsägare* (manager and sheriff) on her own for nearly a decade—a massive job, especially for a single woman—until her death sometime after 1498.

Yet even in death, Brita acted defiantly against the wishes of the Swedish crown, causing a huge who-gets-what hullabaloo by bequeathing the last of her Swedish estates to both Uppsala Cathedral in 1475 *and* the Swedish regent on the order of the court and her relatives in 1484. Which just proves that even though a lot of her documents might have been fake, when it came to holding her own against the patriarchal laws of the land, Brita Tott was the real deal.

Mary
BOWSER

born ca. 1841

AMERICAN SPY

*"I felt that I had the advantage . . .
and that it was my duty if possible to
work where I am most needed."*

Mary Bowser was so good at espionage that, to this day, we
know almost nothing about her. What historians do know
is that she existed (probably); she operated under three
different pseudonyms in Virginia in the 1860s (also probably); she
got married (Once? Twice? Probably twice. Maybe.); and she had
a photographic memory (*definitely* maybe). Oh, and the shadowy
photo that comes up when you google her name? *That's not even
her.* Despite the hazy details, however, when we piece together all
the widely contested and conflicting evidence, a picture (or, okay, a
mosaic) does form, and it looks something like this.

Mary was likely born a slave around 1841 near Richmond,
Virginia. Of her birth family we know little, but she was probably
purchased by a Southern family called the Van Lews to serve as a
companion for their daughter Elizabeth. "Bet" (as Elizabeth was
called) and her parents must have noticed early on that there was
something special about Mary because in May 1846, Mary Jane,
"a colored child belonging to Mrs. Van Lew," was baptized at St.
John's Episcopal church. Most enslaved Africans in Virginia were
baptized at Richmond's First African Baptist Church, but the Van
Lews were no ordinary Virginia family: they were abolitionists and
pro-Unionists hiding in plain sight in the middle of the American

South. When Bet's father died, her family freed their workers (or tried to, since Virginia law, and her father's will, made it virtually impossible to grant slaves freedom) and Mary was taken north to be educated, though it's unclear exactly where. In the vast majority of the South at that time, it was illegal for slaves even to be literate.

A few years later, the Van Lews decided that fourteen-year-old Mary, then going by Mary Jane Richards, would be happiest living outside the United States. Hoping she would use her education to become a missionary—without asking Mary how *she* felt about that—the family helped her board a ship to Monrovia, Liberia, an American colony in Africa established for freed slaves by a group called the American Colonization Society (ACS). (The ACS probably thought this was a great idea, but a bunch of white slave owners deciding to make a freed-slave utopia in Africa will never end well.) After Mary spent five miserable years in the disease-ridden, unfamiliar land, the Van Lews became aware that she hated her life overseas; she returned to Baltimore, thanks to a special request from Bet to the ACS. Mary made the 125-day voyage in steerage (against Bet's wishes that she travel first class) and, after landing in Baltimore, headed back to Richmond—a bold move considering free Black people were 100% unwelcome in Virginia (and *educated* free Black people were about 1000% unwelcome). Sure enough, Mary was arrested in August for traveling on her own without identification papers—but she didn't go submissively. She gave the cops the names "Mary Jones" and "Mary Jane Henley," instead of her real name to avoid harsher punishment, and sat in jail for nine days until Bet arrived to bail her out, claiming that Mary wasn't *technically* a free woman and paying ten bucks for her release. Mary then headed home with Bet . . . probably. The 1860 census tells us that the only free Black servant in the Van Lew household was a "Mary Jones." Then there's the recorded marriage of a Mary, "colored servan[t] to Mrs. E. L. Van Lew," to a man named Wilson Bowser one day before Virginia seceded from the Union—but then we never hear a word about him again. *So what is the truth?*

In short: it's complicated. For one thing, Bet Van Lew wasn't just an abolitionist—she was a spymaster. During the war, she ran one of the most comprehensive railroad and espionage rings in the South. Carefully maintaining a wacky public persona (talking to herself, spacing out, and so on), so-called Crazy Bet was in fact helping Union soldiers escape from prison, using men and women—Black and white alike—to gather sensitive information that she would then send in code to the Union general. It was dangerous work that needed top-notch operatives—and wouldn't you know it, Bet had an educated and super-smart candidate in Mary. Not only was Mary sharp and sly, but she could also work "invisibly" as a domestic servant in white households. Who would suspect that the enslaved woman serving you dinner would later be in your dressing room, memorizing your battle maps and secret letters and sending all that information to the enemy?

Well, definitely not the Confederate States of America president Jefferson Davis. When Davis and his wife set up the Confederate White House in Richmond in 1861, they brought on enslaved workers—among them, possibly, Mary. From that post, she apparently sent Northern leaders as much military information as she could . . . "apparently," because we lack an ironclad source to verify the facts. Thomas McNiven, a Richmond baker who claimed his business was a major hub for the Van Lew spy ring, did say that Mary "had a photographic mind" and "could repeat word for word" everything she heard in the Davis household—which is awesome, except that his claim was recorded in 1952 by Robert Waitt, who heard the story from his aunt Jeanette, who heard it from her father, Thomas McNiven. In other words, not exactly from the horse's mouth.

Still, we do have a more reliable primary source that records details of Mary's key role. Bet reported in her diary that Mary was the one she would ask for news each morning. In addition, in July 1900 an elderly Bet spoke to a reporter for the *Richmond and Manchester Evening Leader* about one of her (unnamed) maids: the woman had been educated in the North, lived in Liberia, and then returned to Richmond to work as a domestic slave—and spy—in the Confederate White House. Sounds an awful lot like Mary, a suggestion further confirmed by a June 1911 article in *Harper's*, for which Bet's niece Annie (only ten years old during the Civil War) gave an interview, corroborated by Bet's journal, saying that this maid of "unusual intelligence" was named Mary Elizabeth Bowser, and that she "was installed as a waitress in the White House of the Confederacy."

Perhaps most convincing is that Mary reported on some of her best spy moments in her own words. In various letters and speeches after the Civil War, Mary mentioned exploits that included sneaking into a secret session of the Rebel Senate, capturing Confederate officers, helping imprisoned Union soldiers, even tracking down smuggled tobacco. Again, not a lot of these details are verifiable— that is, we can't say for sure exactly where Mary was, what she did, or how she pulled it all off—but that's pretty much the standard MO of being a good spy.

Described by newspaper articles and in friends' journal entries as "very sarcastic and at times quite humorous" and "quite a character," Mary spent her life after the war traveling the country, giving speeches and lectures about her time in the South as a "detective" and "secret service" agent. To protect her identity, Mary spoke under false names (like "Richmonia Richards" and "Richmonia R. St. Pierre") and changed details of her history, sometimes claiming she was sold to the Van Lews after returning from Liberia, or giving mixed accounts of her parentage. She taught freed slaves across the South under the alias Mary J. R. Richards, established her own freedman's school in Georgia, and remained fearful of white

Southerners, who had "that sinister expression about the eye, and the quiet but bitterly expressed feeling that I know portends evil," as she wrote in one of her letters to the superintendent of education for the Georgia Freedmen's Bureau, with whom she corresponded while teaching in the state. In 1867 she wrote to the superintendent, with whom she corresponded while teaching in the state, that she had married a man with the surname Garvin who was working in Cuba; her final letter to him says that she planned on leaving the South since her husband was "in the West Indies." And then we never hear from her again.

Nevertheless, some of the most widely reported "facts" about Mary are patently untrue. No primary sources indicate that she ever went by the name "Ellen Bond." It's unlikely she kept a diary that was later lost by the Bowser family, especially since Mary ditched that particular surname and remarried. Jefferson Davis's wife never recalled an educated slave in her household (but then she probably wouldn't, would she?), and Mary probably didn't try to burn down the Confederate White House in 1865, an oft-cited tale published in countless books and articles but having no basis in the historical record (she was teaching in Richmond at that time). But who gives a good gosh-darn? All those myths aside, Mary was still one of the most consistently brave women of the Civil War, and it's a shame we don't know more about how *she* felt instead of how those around her felt *about* her. What was it like to be free in name only, technically still the "property" of Bet, the woman who cared about her and funded her education? What was it like to take down the Confederacy by being a part of the very institution that denied her own humanity? We'll never know Mary's answers to these questions, but we can honor the sacrifice of the many amazing Black female spies in the Civil War by every once in a while remembering the incredibleness of Mary (Jane Elizabeth Richmonia Jones Henley St. Pierre Garvin) Bowser.

Sarah Emma EDMONDS

1841–1898

CANADIAN SOLDIER AND SPY

"I probably drew from [my mother's] breast with my daily food my love of independence and hatred of male tyranny."

Becoming a soldier might not sound like the geekiest calling, especially if, growing up, you were more into reading stuff than stabbing stuff. But becoming a soldier because you read about an awesome lady pirate in a book? One of us, one of us! Meet Sarah Emma Edmonds, the baddest bookish lady ever to take up arms.

The book that helped Emma discover her calling was Maturin Murray Ballou's 1844 novel *Fanny Campbell, the Female Pirate Captain: A Tale of the Revolution*, the thrilling account of a British heroine who dons a sensible pair of trousers and sets out on the wild seas to rescue the love of her life, captured overseas during the American Revolution. (I know—it's so Alanna of Tortall!) Emma tore through the book, and she was pumped about it: "Each exploit of the heroine thrilled me to my finger tips," she later recalled. "I went home that night with the problem of my life solved. I felt equal to the emergency. I was emancipated, and could never be a slave again. When I read where 'Fanny' cut off her brown curls and donned the blue jacket, and stepped into the freedom and glorious independence of masculinity, I threw up my old straw hat and shouted."

Emma had a good reason to desire a little escapism. She

grew up the youngest of four girls in a farming family from New Brunswick, Canada, and since her dad had always wanted a boy (cue groaning), he was not the most thrilled with her arrival. When her parents did eventually have a son, things got even tougher after the boy showed signs of epilepsy. Though Emma had been educated a bit at grammar school, she found herself picking up the "man slack" by taking on the responsibilities of running the homestead, learning how to ride, hunt, shoot, chop wood, forage for food, even how to manage a household and nurse the sick.

As a reward for all her hard work, Emma's father decided that, at the ripe old age of seventeen, she needed to marry the old guy next door because . . . he also owned a farm. Entirely disgusted by the idea, Emma (with the help of her mother and her best friend Linus, who may have hooked her up with some sweet duds) snuck out amid wedding preparations in the middle of the night and ran to a neighboring town. She learned millinery, worked in a hat shop, and all was going great—until her mother alerted her that dear old dad had found out where she was. So Emma, that clever bookish gal, took a cue from her literary heroine, Fanny: she chopped off her hair, threw on some pants, had a telltale mole removed from her left cheek, and high-tailed it to a new town as the newly christened "Franklin Thompson." (And when I say "moved to a new town," I mean just up and walked the 450 miles to Connecticut.)

As Franklin, Emma experienced firsthand all the fantastic freedom she had felt while reading *Fanny Campbell*. Suddenly she could get a job (as a Bible salesman for a large publisher in Nova Scotia, eventually); go out unescorted, even at night; and eat in a restaurant by herself. Understandably, Emma loved her life as a dude, and she was darn good at her job to boot. As her company's top salesman, she could now afford nice clothes and a carriage to take "lady friends out riding occasionally" and, as she put it, have "a nice time generally." As it turned out, though, Bible selling wasn't the steadiest work, since people don't constantly need a whole lot of Bibles. (They're not iPhones, you know? Once you have one, you're good for pretty much forever.) So with only five dollars to her name, Franklin headed out to start a new life in Michigan—though she "came near marrying a pretty little girl who was bound that I should not leave Nova Scotia without her." (Oh, hey! Just gals bein' pals!)

It was in Flint that Emma heard of President Lincoln's call for seventy-five thousand men to fight for the cause of uniting the country in the Civil War. On May 25, 1861, at just twenty years old, she joined up with Company F of the Second Michigan Volunteer Infantry Regiment. How'd she pull it off? Well, given that so many guys were enlisting simultaneously, the medical intake procedures were a bit lax (i.e., if you had ten fingers, ten toes, and most of your teeth, you were good to go). Accustomed to dressing and behaving like Franklin, Emma had no problem fitting in with her division. She was assigned to be a field nurse and mail carrier and took part in a ton of terrifying, unforgiving battles against the Confederates, racing across battlefields covered in blood to give soldiers aid (or brandy) as they lay wounded on the muddy ground.

But nursing wasn't enough for Emma. One of the Union's spies had been captured by the Confederates and subsequently executed—a now-vacant position that needed filling. Eager to get her espionage on, Emma/Franklin submitted to a bunch of tests designed to challenge her values as well as her military knowledge, including a phrenological examination—that thing where they read the bumps on her head to see if the ones that corresponded to her "secretiveness and combativeness" were large enough. She passed muster, but her superiors were unsure if she would be any good at disguise. (Ridiculously ironic, given that no one, not even her tentmate or a fellow soldier she'd known in Canada, had yet figured out her true identity.) To prove her skills, Emma left camp for three days and came back with a completely altered appearance, introducing herself as "Cuff," a Black man (a problematic, but effective, disguise). No one in camp had any idea who she was, and so she got the job. Emma would later infiltrate enemy lines undercover as an enslaved man named Ned, a female Irish pie seller named Bridget O'Shea, a Black laundrywoman, and more. She consistently maintained her disguise, even under duress, allowing her to obtain official papers and information about military numbers, formation, and strategy (including that the Confederates were using "Quaker guns," or big logs painted like cannons, to appear better armed than they were).

Even surrounded by men, Emma still managed to support her fellow ladies and develop female friendships (as should we all!). Already close with a Mrs. B, one of the first and only female front-line nurses in the Civil War and her "constant companion," Emma even befriended women across enemy lines. While on a supply run (aka begging Confederate plantation owners for stuff for the Union army, yikes), Emma found herself invited into the home of a Confederate lady, Alice, who packed Emma a nice basket and showed her on her way—only to up and try to *shoot her in the back*. Undaunted, Emma ducked over her horse's neck, whipped around in her saddle, and returned fire at Alice, nailing her clean through the palm of the hand she'd raised in surrender. Emma then tied Alice's wrist to the back of her horse and dragged her several feet until she apologized, at which point Emma let her ride on her horse back to the Union camp, giving her water and even catching her when she fainted from *being shot in the hand*. When they reached camp, a distraught Alice revealed that she had just lost her father, husband, and two brothers to the war—but instead of resisting, she begged Emma to let her help the Union cause. Over the next few years, Alice—who took the name Nellie—"became one of the most faithful and efficient nurses in the army" and Emma's "faithful friend and companion, my colleague when on duty, and my escort on all occasions in my rides and rambles. She was a splendid woman, and had the best faculty of dispelling the blues, dumps and dismals of any person I ever met."

But life as a soldier in the Union army wasn't all Yankee bro-fists and campfire songs. Emma was still human, and she didn't let her whole "I'm a dude" act stop her from falling in love. In October 1861 she developed a hardcore thing for Jerome Robbins, an assistant surgeon who was in love with another woman. Robbins called his relationship with Franklin "the friendship of one true heart," but after Emma pulled the big reveal (along the lines of "I'm a girl and I love you!"), he rejected her. After her confession, Jerome noted, puzzled, that Emma acted "strangely," "disagreeable," and "very much out of humor" toward him (thereby proving that men two hundred years ago were just as obtuse as they are today). Still, Jerome never revealed Emma's secret, even after he suspected she'd moved on to the handsome (and married) assistant adjutant general James Reid.

Worse than the heartache, though, were the disease and ill health that caused more battlefield deaths than the actual combat. Nasty things like dysentery, diarrhea, and dehydration were rampant in camps constantly battered by wind and rain, and nurses and surgeons were barely trained to care for the ill. Emma had suffered from a broken leg, a horse bite, a lung hemorrhage, malaria (which she contracted while delivering letters across a buggy swamp), and what was likely posttraumatic stress disorder after a shell exploded in front of her tent. With all those injuries adding up, Emma realized she *really* needed medical attention or she would be on the fast track to corpse town. Denied leave for medical aid and fearing that a military doctor would poke around and discover her secret (we've all seen *Mulan*), on April 19, 1863, Emma took off for a civilian hospital in Ohio, planning to return to her unit after she'd recovered. By the time she left the hospital, however, Franklin Thompson had been labeled a deserter—meaning she'd be put to death if she returned to battle. Instead, "with much reluctance," Emma threw on a dress, resumed her real name, and volunteered as a nurse at a Christian Commission hospital in Harpers Ferry, West Virginia.

It was during this time that she also penned her war memoirs, *Unsexed; or, The Female Soldier*, later retitled *Nurse and Spy in the Union Army*. Published by the same folks for whom she used to sell Bibles, the book was a massive success, selling nearly 200,000 copies (a lot for a book today, let alone in the 1860s); it is the only evidence we have of Emma's time as a spy, since no official government records corroborate her claims. But most historians agree that Emma was on the level about most of her tales, even if she exaggerated some of her story for entertainment value. You might begrudgingly think, "well, a girl's gotta eat," but Emma didn't even keep most earnings from her book sales. She donated the majority of the profits to war aid efforts, including the United States Sanitary Commission, newly founded by none other than Emily and Elizabeth Blackwell (remember them from chapter 2?).

After the war (and by complete fluke), Emma ran into her old hometown friend Linus, who was then a carpenter in West Virginia. After three years of correspondence, they married—Emma liked that Linus was from home and that he never judged her for her exploits. Moving constantly across the United States in pursuit of work, the couple had three children, none of whom lived past age six, and subsequently adopted two boys they raised as their own. Emma enrolled at Oberlin College but hated it (not to put too fine a point on it). She'd never really gotten over being labeled a deserter. She knew she deserved a military pension, but she also knew it would be difficult to convince the government she truly had fought in the war (even though it's probable that nearly four hundred women were active in the Civil War). So she did the most dramatic thing possible: at a reunion of her Michigan Infantry division, she showed up in full skirts and was like, "Hey guys, it's me, Franklin!" Everyone was utterly confused until her colonel admitted, "I recall many things which ought to have betrayed her, except that no one thought of finding a woman in a soldier's dress."

Getting over the initial shock (and acting way cooler about the situation than one would anticipate), Emma's fellow veterans submitted to Congress all kinds of praise on her behalf, saying that (as Franklin) she had "performed cheerfully and fully and at all times any duty which was assigned her," that "more than one member of the company can attest to the care, kindness and self-sacrificing devotion of 'Frank' to the sick soldiers of the regiment," and that she "rode with a fearlessness that attracted the attention and secured the commendation of field and general officers." Her old captain (the one who mistakenly admitted her into the army; awkward) even said that she "won the respect, admiration, and confidence of both officers and men." The secretary of war then verified that Emma was "a female soldier who served as a private—rendering faithful service in the ranks." In 1884 Congress passed a bill allowing her to receive a $12 monthly pension, $100 in back pay (over $300 and $2,500, respectively, in Today Dollars), and an honorable discharge. Two years later, her desertion charge was expunged.

Finally settling in Texas, Emma became the only woman admitted to the Grand Army of the Republic, the Civil War Union Army veterans' organization. She died on September 5, 1898, at age fifty-nine. Her coffin was carried by delegates from the Grand Army, and she is the only woman buried in a cemetery plot reserved for veterans of the Civil War—an ending that would make even Fanny Campbell proud.

Elvira
CHAUDOIR

1913–
1995

PERUVIAN HEIRESS AND SPY

I t's unfair when people underestimate the intelligence of a woman just because she likes to go out and party. Not every nerd prefers to spend downtime alone in front of a video game or curled up with a comic book; some of us like to recharge our brain batteries by going out and socializing with people—socializing with, slash spying on. Which brings us to one Elvira Concepción Josefina de la Fuente Chaudoir.

Elvira grew up in Paris, where she enjoyed a pretty posh lifestyle. Her dad was rolling in fertilizer money (not *literally*, though, because ew) and had been assigned as the Peruvian chargé d'affaires (like an ambassador) to the Vichy regime set up by the Germans in France. Highly educated and openly bisexual, Elvira had twice the brains of everyone around her and was consistently bored with a life that didn't offer her much opportunity to use them. At age twenty-three she eloped with the Belgian stock trader Jean Chaudoir. Four years and many affairs later, she realized that she had "nothing in common with her husband" and bailed to the south of France with her (super-rich by marriage) best girlfriend. The two of them partook in Elvira's favorite activity—losing at gambling—until the Germans invaded, prompting Elvira to jump in a convertible and head for England. There she found herself at loose ends: she was almost broke (despite trying her best to gamble her way into some money) and summarily rejected from a government job. When she failed to hold down a translating gig at the BBC, she ended up spending most of her time hanging out drinking at the Ritz. One day she happened to complain about her financial and fun-times woes to the right person—an RAF officer—and shortly thereafter came face-to-face with the assistant chief of MI6.

Lieutenant Colonel Claude Edward Marjoribanks Dansey not only had the most British name ever to Brit but was also described by one wartime historian as "corrupt, incompetent, but with a certain low cunning." Nevertheless, Dansey knew the value of a smart woman whom other people assumed to be stupid, and he was well aware of Elvira's debts—around a thousand pounds (nearly sixty thousand dollars today). In fact, he knew so much about her life that Elvira was pretty sure he'd been tapping her phone. Put that together with an impressive circle of wealthy, important friends and a Peruvian diplomatic passport, and Dansey had a hunch Elvira would make the perfect secret agent—he hoped the Germans would think so, too. In return for one hundred pounds a month, Elvira was to wander around the South of France doing pretty much what she would be doing otherwise—playing bridge poorly and drinking— until a German Abwehr (secret service) agent inevitably approached her with a similar offer, a process called "coat-tailing." Money and a chance to use her wits? Obviously, Elvira was instantly down.

So in 1942, at age twenty-nine, Elvira stocked up on invisible ink to use in passing messages back to England and got busy doin' her thing (which was, again, being *really* terrible at gambling, but now with the British government's money). Dansey knew he'd put his faith in the right woman. Sure, MI6 worried about the huge, raucous parties she threw and the potential of blackmail over her "Lesbian tendencies" (the MI6 files always capitalize *Lesbian* when they talk about her, as if they thought she was from the island of

Lesbos). Her MI6 assessment said she was a "member of the inter-national smart gambling set" who was "very intelligent and quick to grasp essentials" and had "a quick brain but is probably rather lazy about using it." Surveillance said she preferred the "high spots"; police said "drunken men and women in the small hours" showed up at her apartment all the time. Deputy Chief Constable Joseph Goulder noted that she "favors the companionship of women who may not be careful of their virginity." But ultimately MI6 knew Elvira was never sympathetic to the Germans and that all these things were to their advantage. Smart boys.

Finally, after months without a bite (during which time Elvira started to tire of the "people who get all the food they want, who wear lovely clothes, and who, though dancing is forbidden even to them, spend their nights gambling in the casinos" in the midst of a war), Elvira was approached at a Cannes casino by a Nazi collabo-rator named Henri Chauvel, and she went to *work*. He introduced her to his German friend Helmut "Bibi" Bleil, a freelance spy. After a week of charming Bibi over dinners and moaning about her fi-nancial hardships (which, true, but still), Elvira finally got an in when Bibi asked if, hey, maybe you could move back to England, and my friends will pay you eighty-eight pounds a month disguised as alimony from your ex-husband if you let us know what's goin' on back in Britain? Heck, *yes*, Elvira said. Bibi gave her a code name, Dorette, and a bottle of German invisible ink, talking it up as the greatest invention in the world. "You will have to be terribly careful and never tell a soul about it," Bibi said. "Because, if you do, you will be the first to pay. . . . I always act on intuition, and I feel I can just trust you. If I am wrong, it will ruin my whole career."

He was, and it did. Elvira immediately informed MI6 what was going on, and just like that she became part of an elaborate network of spies across Europe called the Double-Cross System or, even radder, the XX System (it's two crosses, see). Overseen by the so-called Twenty Committee (Roman numeral humor!), the system took Nazi spies—who were typically not people like Elvira, but rather Germans who had either been captured or willingly turned themselves in—and made them into double agents who could then be used to feed the Nazis misinformation. Elvira's MI6 case officers Christopher Harmer and Hugh Astor gave her the code name "Bronx," for the cocktail she would drink when meeting with them. Elvira, a "very competent letter-writing agent," sent letters ostensibly full of girly mundanities (like, you know, make-up and stuff, I guess) to the Banco Santo Espirito in Lisbon, which would transfer them to Bibi. Between the lines, in invisible ink, she would give the Germans just enough false information to steer them wrong without arousing suspicion—for example, thwarting gas attacks by telling them how ready Britain was for retaliation, mixed in with things like "Shortage of kitchen utensils." She kept all this from her girlfriend Monica Sheriffe, who was a racehorse owner and never knew a thing about Elvira's job.

But the Germans were getting anxious. They knew an invasion was planned; they just didn't know when. Since the mail was so slow, they came up with a faster way for Elvira (whom they trusted as one of their most "reliable agents") to get them information: she would send a money order to her Lisbon bank, and its wording would indicate the details of the attack. "Send 80 pounds which I need for my dentist" would mean the attack would be on the Atlantic in a week's time; thirty pounds would mean Denmark, ten the Balkans, and so on. As part of "Operation Fortitude," an XX System plan to divert Nazi attention from the real invasion at Normandy, Elvira, being the most clever, sent a telegram asking for fifty pounds, indicating the Bay of Biscay, along with a letter describing how she'd wheedled the information out of a certain drunk RAF captain (whom she'd never met IRL and who barely even drank in the first place). When the boats landed in Normandy, an entire German tank division was chilling in the Bay of Biscay, doing not a dang thing. D-Day was a success.

Elvira continued to love life the most, and the Germans continued to trust her—even *after* D-Day! When in 1944 the Nazis failed to meet her as agreed in Madrid (a meeting at which she might have been interrogated about the whole Bay of Biscay incident), she wrote them the angriest, most spoiled entitled-girl letter that has likely ever been penned: "Absolutely livid about the uselessness of the journey which was expensive and disagreeable. You let me down." To the Nazis! Who then *apologized* and asked very nicely to keep working with her! What a queen.

After the war, Elvira lived out the next fifty years in the south of France, running a gift shop and living off her inheritance—which would run dry by 1995. A month before her death, however, she received a five-thousand-pound check in the mail from the director general of MI5. Sometimes all you need to know is that you're still appreciated. And that not every geeky gal is an introvert. Or, you know, good at counting cards.

Noor
INAYAT KHAN

1914–
1944

INDIAN AMERICAN AUTHOR AND ALLIED SPY

"The people of all the kingdoms loved each other, and they all lived happily ever after."

Nothing is more devastating than making it all the way through an awesome story only to find out the protagonist dies before the ultimate victory. So here is the truth: on September 13, 1944, a woman named Noor Inayat Khan was shot in the back of the head by Nazis at Dachau concentration camp. Her last word before execution, defiant in the face of one of the evilest forces the world has ever known, was "*Liberté*!" But just because Noor didn't live to a ripe old age (or live to see the memorial bust in her likeness that now resides in London) doesn't mean that her story is any less incredible, or that we should be any less stoked about it.

Noor was truly a woman of the world. Her father was Indian royalty and her mother was an American commoner; the couple met in Russia and raised their children in France. On her father's side, Noor's great-great-great grandfather was Tipu Sultan, the ruler of the Indian kingdom of Mysore (and also the guy who so hated the British colonizing his country that he teamed up with Napoleon to keep them out). A century later, Noor's father rejected the militaristic world climate and chose instead to travel the globe as a teacher and practitioner of the mystical beliefs of Sufism, an esoteric offshoot of Islam characterized by asceticism. It was on one such lecture trip to San Francisco that he met Ora Ray Baker, the woman who would become Noor's mother. After their marriage in 1913, Noor's mother took the name Ameena Begum and, in January 1914, gave birth to little Noor-un-Nisa (meaning "light of womanhood") in St. Petersburg.

The family settled near Paris, in a home that would become a central meeting place of the local Sufi order. Though Noor grew up one of five siblings, she excelled in her own right. After her father died unexpectedly on a trip to India in 1927, Noor took over as head of household but still managed to earn two degrees, one in psychobiology of the child (at the Sorbonne) and one in harp (at the Paris Conservatory). Above all else, though, Noor loved children, and in 1939 she wrote an adorable illustrated children's book called *Twenty Jataka Tales* (which you can read online). She infused the book with the pacifist morality she had learned from her father, with tales like "The Baby Quail and the Wood Fire," which instructs readers how to stand up to those who would hurt your family, and "The Sarabha," which teaches nonviolence toward living things.

So when war broke out and the Germans occupied France, Noor—being pretty keen on the whole "practice what you preach" concept—knew she couldn't just sit around while the Nazis stormed their way across Europe. But she was conflicted; like her several-times-great grandfather before her, she was *not* a big fan of England because of the country's colonization of India. Still, she reasoned that maybe, if an Indian were to perform an epic service for England, relations might improve between the two countries—or, as her brother would phrase it in 2003, "thwart the aggression of the tyrant." "I wish some Indians would win high military distinction in this war," said Noor. "If one or two could do something in the Allied service which was very brave and which everybody admired it would help to make a bridge between the English people and the Indians." If only someone could summon the steely resolve necessary to undertake this task, Noor! Could it be . . . you?

In 1940 Noor bravely signed up for the British Women's Auxiliary Air Force and was accepted under the name Nora Baker (despite telling WAAF officers that after World War II she might head to India to kick the British out of her country. They may have been afraid of her). She trained as a wireless operator, one of the most difficult wartime jobs, which she rocked thanks to her musician-y fingers. But boring ol' Morse code wasn't enough for Noor, and so when she saw a posting inviting personnel who could speak fluent French and were skilled at wireless to apply for "special duties," she leapt at the chance. As you may have guessed, the special duties turned out to be service in the Special Operations Executive, aka the British double-secret-probation spy division. The SOE fake-enrolled Noor in FANY, or First Aid Nursing Yeomanry (thinking that Germans might be nicer to captured female spies if they thought the women were nurses), and shipped her all over the country to learn how to be the best wireless-operator secret agent she could possibly be.

Not surprisingly, almost all of Noor's male supervisors underestimated her skill and talent. *Some* were positive: her intake officer, the novelist Selwyn Jepson, said that he had "not the slightest doubt" that Noor, with her "fine spirit," would make a great agent; and her cryptography teacher, Leo Marks, reported that "Madeleine" (Noor's code name) could transpose "flawless" messages in record time (he even used metaphors from Noor's own book to help her make sense of the complicated codes). But everybody else . . . not so much. Her clandestinity tutor said she was "too emotional and impulsive to be suitable for employment as a secret agent" because she was "too sensitive and easily hurt." Another called her a "vague, dreamy creature, far too conspicuous," who was scared of weapons and was so clumsy she couldn't even jump. The superintendent who mock-interrogated her said, "If this girl's an agent, I'm Winston Churchill." (That's not even a good burn.) Noor's Special Operations Executive finishing report called her "not over-burdened with brains" and possessed of "an unstable and temperamental personality" that made it "very doubtful whether she is really suited to work in the field." Lesson being: even if you are the best at what you do in the entire world (and, trust, Noor was up there), some jerks will always try to make you feel bad about your abilities.

Anyway, the SOE's military need for operatives outweighed their patriarchal desire to feel superior to this lovely Indian gal, and they sent Noor into action, making her the first female wireless operator dispatched to France. Now she was known as Jeanne-Marie Regnier, a governess from Blois, who had been given two suitcases (one containing her wireless), a broad spectrum of pills (including one that would kill her in case of capture), and a six-week life expectancy. Noor landed on a secret runway in the middle of the night with her associates (two women on her spy team, a courier and an organizer), and then headed alone to Paris. Upon arriving at her handler's house, she told him she hadn't eaten since leaving England because no one had taught her how to use her confusing ration book—but she *had* brought him carnations. Next, Jeanne-Marie convinced her *German* neighbor to help set up her wireless antenna by craftily telling him it was a clothesline.

But not everything was so simple. In addition to missing her mother (who thought her daughter was on vacation in Africa), Noor soon faced dire circumstances: within a few weeks of her arrival in Paris, the Sicherheitsdienst (or SD, the SS intelligence agency) had arrested Noor's entire spy ring—not just the two girls she arrived with, but practically every British undercover agent in Paris. British Intelligence told Noor to lie low, but she refused to stop broadcasting and wouldn't leave her post without a replacement. So for nearly four months, Noor was basically in charge of British secret communications in Paris. To keep the Germans off her trail, she dyed her hair and traveled from safe house to safe house. When transmitting critical encoded information back to England, she could broadcast for no longer than twenty minutes at a time lest she risk detection by the German's sneaky mobile wireless detectors. In fact, Noor was Number 1 on the SD's Most Wanted List, and they knew nearly everything about her, from her code name to her likeness. But they couldn't stop a girl with a mission. Noor's perseverance saw her through many tricky operations, including helping in the escape of thirty airmen who had been shot down.

Tragically, in October 1943 Noor was betrayed—possibly by a double agent—and captured by the Germans. During her imprisonment, she told the Gestapo nothing, not even her name (though they did find a notebook in which she had written her communications, probably because of a misunderstanding during her rushed training). Even braver, Noor twice attempted escape, first by trying to climb out a bathroom window within minutes of arriving at her first prison, and second by unscrewing the bars on her cell's skylight, hiding the plaster damage with makeup (!), and tying together sheets and blankets to form a rope that allowed her to reach the building next door. She almost got away with it, too, but was thwarted, ironically, by the increased security brought on by a British air raid. She ended up shackled in solitary confinement as a "highly dangerous" prisoner after refusing to sign a paper saying she would never again try to flee. A year later, right before the end of the war—well, go reread the first paragraph. It didn't end well for our Noor, but she fought until the bitter end.

In 1949, five years after her death, Noor was awarded the George Cross, Britain's highest honor for heroism in the face of extreme danger, and was recognized in a newspaper article as "the first woman operator to be infiltrated into enemy occupied France" who "refused however to abandon what had become the principal and most dangerous post in France." In France, where every year a military band still plays in her honor on her home street, Noor was given a similar military decoration, the Croix de Guerre with gilt star (an extra pin to mark that she had been mentioned in an official report by a superior officer). In 2011 Noor's biographer started a campaign to raise money to erect a bronze bust of her likeness in George Square Gardens in London. A year later, Princess Anne revealed a memorial in front of hundreds of Noor's family members and former SOE coworkers, making Noor the first Muslim or Asian woman ever to have a memorial in all of Britain.

Noor was so kind to everyone that even the Gestapo officer in charge of her imprisonment was moved by her death. When he heard the news after the war, he broke down in tears. As her brother Vilayat noted, "All those who knew her had a deep respect for her whilst being moved by some endearing feature of her being. Was it because she so deeply cared for all those she came across—even her jailers?" More than likely. We should all be so brave.

SMUGGLERS, SECRET AGENTS, AND NINJAS

Other Amazing Women of Espionage

MOCHIZUKI CHIYOME

ACTIVE CA. 1561 Widowed in 1561 during Japan's Warring States period, Chiyome kept busy by starting a home for wayward girls in Nagano prefecture, ostensibly for teaching them to become Shinto shrine maidens. Instead, Chiyome—who may have been descended from a legendary leader of the Kōga-ryū school of *ninjutsu*—turned the girls into "*kunoichi*," or bad-as-hell secret agents. The girls gathered intelligence, made split-second situation analyses, and were well versed in the arts of disguise, manipulation, rumor spreading, and behavior modification. They were also pretty fearsome fighters: trained in lightning-fast combat with staves, canes, knives, spears, swords, even their bare hands, the girls used their smaller, more lithe frames to their advantage against large male opponents. Thus prepped, *kunoichi* could infiltrate the homes of high-ranking men as maids, geisha, or friends in ways that no other spy could. Black Widow, eat your heart out.

CHARLOTTE DE SAUVE

1551–1617 You might know of the super-powerful Catherine de' Medici—but did you know she had a group of lady spies called *L'escadron volant* (The Flying Squadron), whose sole purpose was to seduce important court dudes and then report juicy details back to the queen? Well, she absolutely did (although their femme fatale-ness was almost certainly blown out of proportion by misogynists upset with women in court gaining power), and Charlotte de Sauve was one such woman in Catherine's care. Charlotte went after King Henry of Navarre, using her wiles to become his confidante and eventually wielding a huge amount of influence over him—all likely at Catherine's behest. But she didn't stop there: Charlotte would go on to seduce Navarre's brother-in-law François, too, spurring a fight between the two men over her affections.

APHRA BEHN

C. 1640–1689 Most famous for her writing (perhaps you've heard of her novel *Oroonoko*), Aphra Behn was also a super-radical super-spy. Since she never really stuck to the same story, we don't know much about her childhood (spies, sheesh), but we do know that she had become involved with King Charles II's court by 1665, when the Second Anglo-Dutch War between England and the Netherlands had started to go down. In Antwerp, it is believed that Aphra was given the code name Astrea and became a spy for the English court. Eventually, in need of money, Aphra became a scribe for the King's Company, with her subsequent prolific writing career cementing her place in history as one of England's first professional female writers.

CHEVALIER D'ÉON

1728–1810 It is impossible to say that the Chevalier d'Éon was a transgender woman, since such terminology didn't exist in eighteenth-century France. We *do* know, however, that the chevalier, though assigned male at birth, spent thirty-three years dressed as a woman and asking to be referred to as such. We also know that in 1756, after graduating law school at age twenty-one, the chevalier joined French king Louis XV's network of super-spies, the Secret du Roi, and eventually claimed to have infiltrated the inner circle of the Russian empress Elizabeth by dressing as a woman named Lia de Beaumont. Despite wagers on the London Stock Exchange about the chevalier's "real" gender (gross), the French government recognized and affirmed the chevalier's identification as a woman, with King Louis XVI even funding a new wardrobe of traditionally feminine clothing for the courtier now known as Madame d'Éon.

MANUELA SÁENZ

1797–1856 *La Conquista*, the Spanish occupation of South America, was truly terrible: colonists held power for centuries with no regard for the land's indigenous people. Spain was pretty big on this system for a long time—but the Venezuelan leader Simón Bolívar was *very* against it. He dedicated his life to establishing sovereignty for Venezuela, Ecuador, Bolivia, Peru, and Colombia—an accomplishment that would have been impossible without Manuela Sáenz. After leaving behind her rich English husband to become a revolutionary, Manuela fell in love with Bolívar in Quito, Ecuador, and went on to help his cause by campaigning for women's rights, operating a spy network, and even saving his life, for which she became known as "the Liberator of the Liberator." She not only fought in the all-important Battle of Ayacucho but also straight-up stripped a dead enemy of his mustache, which she would later carry around and wear to costume parties.

JOSEPHINE BAKER

1906–1975 You probably know this dancer/singer/actress for her infamous banana skirt (or her pet cheetah), but underneath that tasty outfit was a stealthy spy. Born Freda Josephine McDonald in St. Louis, Josephine Baker was an excellent dancer who dropped out of school at age thirteen to perform her act on the streets. Two years later she was hired for vaudeville and quickly became a successful chorus girl in New York City during the Harlem Renaissance. Fluent in French, she danced her way to Paris in 1925 and found huge success there, even becoming the first Black woman to star in a major film (1934's *Zouzou*). When World War II broke out, Josephine turned spy for the Allies, using her invites to fancy parties to chat people up for information about German, Japanese, and Italian war efforts, which she would then pass along to French military intelligence. As a star, she could travel Europe unquestioned and rub elbows with the fanciest of fascists without anyone suspecting her true motives (writing notes in invisible ink on sheet music). After returning to the United States postwar, Josephine—who was biracial and likely bisexual—spent much of her later life fighting for civil rights.

NANCY WAKE

1912–2011 New Zealand–born Nancy Wake was basically a real-life Agent Carter. At age sixteen, she ran away from her school in Sydney, Australia, and headed to London. After some self-tutoring in journalism, she worked for the *Chicago Tribune* as a correspondent in Paris during the rise of Nazi power. Once World War II began, Nancy joined the French Resistance and British Special Operations, smuggling Allied internees and POWs out of France. (She was so good at escaping the Germans—often via flirtation—that the Gestapo started calling her the White Mouse.) By 1943 she was at the top of the Gestapo's most-wanted list, with a five million franc price on her head. But they never caught her—probably because she did things like *kill an SS sentry with her bare hands* to stop him from raising an alarm. Unsurprisingly, Nancy became one of the most heavily decorated servicewomen of World War II.

Q&A WITH
LINDSAY MORAN
AUTHOR, JOURNALIST,
AND FORMER CIA OPERATIVE

Q: *When did you become interested in espionage as a career? Did anyone encourage you?*

I realized from a young age that I wanted to "be a spy." I was obsessed with the fictional character Harriet the Spy and kind of modeled my early life after her. I spied on everyone—my brother, my parents, my neighbors—and took little notes about their activities. I communicated with one of my best friends via secret code, using flashlights in our windows at night. As a teenager, I experimented with alias identities (i.e., fake ID cards) and cover stories. I would not say anyone encouraged me; the desire definitely came from within.

Q: *What difficulties or barriers did you experience in joining and working for the CIA, and how did you overcome them?*

The application, recruitment, and hiring process was incredibly competitive, but I certainly didn't feel at a disadvantage as a woman. In fact, much of being a good spy is being disarming, charming, easy to talk to, a good listener, and empathetic. I found all these traits came naturally to me, perhaps in part because I'm a woman. Men—or at least men attracted to this line of work—may oftentimes let their egos get in the way of sitting back and listening. Perhaps it's sexist to say, but I also think women tend to have more nuanced manipulation skills, a cornerstone to good spying.

What are some of the craziest things you had to learn or do as a CIA spy?

Defensive driving—crashing through barriers with a car; dismantling explosives; jumping out of planes; traveling under an alias and operating in disguise; using weapons; withstanding harsh interrogation. These were all invaluable skills I learned in training. I didn't use all of them in the field; but many I did use, and some (like general situational awareness and surveillance detection) I still rely on today. They become habit.

 If you could time travel, what warnings would you give your younger self about your career path?

I wish I'd told myself not to take the small things—operational hiccups, suffocating bureaucracy—too seriously. Of course, it's a life-and-death game, but spying and espionage can be a lot of fun. I did have fun, but I also internalized a lot of the stress. I wish I'd taken time to relish that I was doing one of the coolest, most important governmental jobs anyone can ever have.

 What has the transition to a career as an author and a journalist been like? What do you most enjoy writing about?

Believe it or not, there's an inordinate amount of paperwork and writing involved in operational activity. That I had a background in writing, enjoy writing, and am good at it helped in my CIA career. Being a journalist is not unlike being a spy. You're trying to get people (sources) to give you information, to tell their story, even if they are reluctant. Of course, as a journalist conducting an interview, you're upfront about whom you work for. But you're still relying on people skills, powers of manipulation, the ability to empathize—all the same skills that I drew on as a spy.

Q: *What advice would you give women who want to break into the world of espionage?*

Wear sensible shoes! No, seriously, I'd say go for it. The CIA might be a good ol' boy network, but in my opinion HUMINT (human intelligence) is largely a woman's world.

> As a CIA operative, **LINDSAY MORAN** faced everything from POW situations to fast-paced car chases. Now working as a writer and journalist, Lindsay is the author of *Blowing My Cover*, an amazing memoir about her time as a CIA spy. Find out more about Lindsay on her website blowingmycover.com, or follow her on Twitter @LindsayMoran.

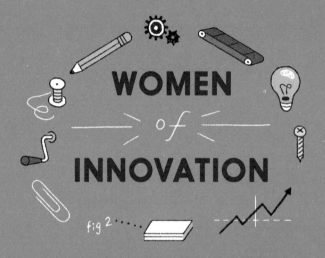

CHAPTER FOUR

WOMEN of INNOVATION

fig 2

"The question is sneeringly asked sometimes, Can a woman invent?" So begins the chapter on inventors in the 1883 book *Women of the Century*. The answer is obviously yes—they can invent anything they want. But still, the facts are bleak. Of the more than five million U.S. patents that have been granted since 1790, only about 5 percent have a woman's name on them. Men often took credit for women's inventions, sometimes at the behest of women of color who feared that white consumers wouldn't want to purchase their items. Women were often denied access to education and tools that made it possible to invent stuff in the first place. And since patents are property, it helps to be able to, you know, *own* property so you can file for one. Let's give a well-deserved deep-knee curtsey to these queens, because they *did* do the things, make the things, and use the things, and all our lives are better for it.

Huang
DAOPO

ca.
1240–
1330

CHINESE TEXTILE PIONEER

"Granny Huang, Granny Huang, teach me spinning, teach me weaving. Turning two spools of yarn into two bolts of cloth."

They say necessity is the mother of invention—and nothing says necessity like "Kublai Khan is invading and everyone I love is poor but still needs clothes." The woman known as Huang Daopo grew up needing many things—not least a better living situation than the abusive foster home in which she grew up. She likely never realized that mustering the bravery to escape would lead her to revitalize an entire industry.

Around 1240 in China, things were getting pretty wild. The Mongol armies of Genghis and Kublai Khan were fighting constantly to take control of the country, and though the millions of people living in cities thrived, residents of farming towns had a way harder time—especially the women. But despite (or perhaps because of) the invasions, the Song dynasty saw much economic and technical advancement. Craftspeople would follow in the steps of the Mongol army, which had entire government offices devoted to watching over and regulating artisan families (though these were often fraught with extortion, leading some families to escape and decentralize).

The weaving industry in particular was big business (people gotta wear clothes, you know), and the Chinese were known for their complex and high-quality brocades. Though everyone wanted some sweet cotton duds, the processes for making them were incredibly inefficient. Weaving required a ton of labor: cloth makers had to clean the seeds out of raw cotton by hand, fluff it by beating the fibers using a bamboo bow fitted with a hammer, and spin it using a slow single-spindle hand-turned spinning wheel. Harder still than producing fabric was *growing enough stuff to eat*, and Songjiang, a town outside what is now Shanghai, was cursed with soil that was too poor to produce food crops, let alone cotton. In a country beset by strife, Songjiang's inhabitants were suffering.

Into this harsh world Huang was born, probably around 1240 or 1245 and likely to an impoverished family, at least according to the late Yuan/early Ming scholar Wang Feng (who calls our heroine "cut from different cloth," because never underestimate the power of puns in any era). Huang was her family name; her first name has been lost to history. Daopo is a later addition, an honorific we might equate to "Auntie Huang" or, more accurately "Huang, crone of the Dao" or "Sister Huang" ("sister" in the nun way). Huang was probably sold to another family in what was called a *shim-pua* marriage—basically an arranged union in which a family with a young boy adopted another family's young daughter (sometimes as early as infancy), engaged the pair, and then raised them together to be married around twelve years old. Known as "little daughter-in-law" or "daughter-in-law raised from a child" (or, let's be honest, "child bride"), girls in these set-ups provided another set of hands, guaranteed a cheap marriage (no bride price for the groom's family to pay), and were thought to produce male offspring. In reality, *shim-pua* marriages were far less likely to be successful than regular marriages because, according to what sociologists call the Westermarck effect, you can't really feel romantic about someone you grew up with like a sibling (unless you're a Lannister or maybe a Winchester). Huang's adoptive family was apparently the absolute worst to her, too. Indeed, mistreatment was common for *shim-pua* girls. Mothers, devastated at having to give away their own babies while raising a stranger's, would work the adopted girls to exhaustion, often failing to provide adequate food or shelter.

So Huang bust out of there, literally. In her midteens (or possibly as young as twelve) she is said to have burst through the thatched roof of her in-laws' home. She then ran as far and as fast as she could, hiding herself in a boat on the Huangpu River—a boat that carried her all the way to Yazhou (modern-day Sanya) on Hainan Island, off the southern coast of China. Hainan Island was home to the ethnic Li (or Hlai) peoples, who had (and still have, in fact) a unique culture and language entirely separate from those of mainland China, including their own ways of cultivating and weaving cotton. Huang lived there for over thirty years, learning Super Effective weaving and spinning skillz. She left the island around 1296, at fifty-ish years old, and returned to her hometown.

But Huang didn't return alone. Not only did she bring back a finer, higher grade of cotton seed that could be grown locally, but she also had in her brain all the amazing Hainan techniques for turning those seeds into shirts. First, she developed a two-roller cotton gin to eliminate seeds from the cotton, which was way faster than picking them by hand. (The Western world wouldn't see anything like it until *five centuries* later, in 1794, when Eli Whitney patented his cotton gin—although he probably got the idea from a woman named Catherine Greene, but that's another, entirely-not-shocking story.) Next, Huang showed the local people a better way of bowing, which used five-foot wooden clappers tied to a wooden bow to untangle and fluff the fiber to prep it for spinning. And then (oh, no, she wasn't done) she made a three-spindle treadle-operated spinning wheel that allowed one person to spin multiple threads at the same time—yet another innovation that wouldn't be seen in Europe until the advent of the spinning jenny in the 1760s. With this wheel, one could make about six ounces of cotton per day, enough to start weaving in just four days.

All this innovation was huge for the town of Songjiang. In his 1366 work *Chuogeng lu* (Writing and Creating), the biographer Tao Zongyi says that Huang took one of the poorest regions in China and made it into one of the most prosperous; suddenly, it was the cotton production capital of the world. Since you need humid weather to weave properly (or the thread gets too brittle and cold) but less humid weather to grow the seeds, northern China would grow all the cotton and ship it down to Songjiang, where it was turned into items like belts, mattresses, handkerchiefs, and the famously gorgeous cotton-silk jacquard quilts made with beautiful interlocking and color matching (sometimes in the widely sought-after "cloud cloth" pattern featuring flowers, phoenixes, and Chinese characters). Surrounded by waterways and lots of people familiar with hemp and silk spinning, Songjiang became a national trading hub, and thousands of people's lives were changed for the better.

Huang became a national hero. Seven years after her death, in 1330, the people around Songjiang collected money to build a shrine in her honor, and "Granny Huang" became the subject of a popular folk song about spinning and cloth making (although no doubt a little something is lost in translation). Her shrine and tomb are now in the Shanghai Botanical Gardens (though the originals were damaged somewhat during the Cultural Revolution), which also hosts a statue of her likeness at the center of a courtyard. The 2010 Chinese miniseries *A Weaver on the Horizon* was (*very loosely*) based on what we know of her life, she's on a Scientists of Ancient China stamp, and she's even got a crater on Venus named after her, which is pretty *out of this world*, if I do say so (like I said, puns rock). And it all started because she had the courage to break out on her own.

Margaret
KNIGHT

1838–1914

AMERICAN INVENTOR

"I'm not surprised at what I've done. I'm only sorry I couldn't have had as good a chance as a boy, and have been put to my trade regularly."

The next time you pick up a tasty burger and the cashier puts your food into a convenient takeaway bag, you have a radical lady named Margaret Knight to thank. No, not for the burger (because that would be a disgustingly old burger), but for the essential invention so commonplace we take it for granted: the humble flat-bottomed paper bag.

Speaking of humble, our story begins in 1838 with a poor family in York, Maine. Margaret Knight was born the youngest of five children, with two older brothers and sisters. After the death of Margaret's father, her widowed mother moved the family to Manchester, New Hampshire, where she put the kids to work in the local cotton mills (this is pre-child-labor laws). Margaret would often visit her older brothers at work, running underfoot (pro tip: *Do not do this in nineteenth-century cotton mills*) to bring her sibs their lunches. It was on one of these visits that twelve-year-old Margaret experienced what she would later call the happiest moment of her entire career: she witnessed a steel-tipped loom shuttle as it fell and injured a worker. (Er, which is *not* the part she liked! Bear with me, here.)

See, young Margaret was already prone to tinkering. Instead of dolls, "the only things I wanted were a jack-knife, a gimlet, and pieces of wood," she once recalled. "My friends were horrified. I was called a tomboy; but that made very little impression on me. . . . I was always making things for my brothers: did they want any thing in the line of playthings, they always said, 'Mattie will make them for us.' I was famous for my kites; and my sleds were the envy and admiration of all the boys in town." With her super-smart inventor-brain in tip-top shape from all that toy inventing, Margaret figured out a way to improve the mill's safety by equipping the shuttles with what was basically an autostop or a cover (depending on which source you believe) so they would no longer be able to injure workers. In the years that followed, her design was implemented at mills across New England.

Despite saving what was probably tons of limbs, Margaret never received a patent for her first invention, but she remained determined to support herself with her big brain. After years of bouncing from job to job in fields like photography, upholstery, and engraving, she eventually found her way to Springfield, Massachusetts, where she got a job at Columbia Paper Bag Company. There she made flat-bottomed bags by hand, earning a paltry $1.50 to $3.50 for a week of ten-hour days (a third less than the men made, of course).

At the time, machines were pretty efficient at whipping up envelope-style paper bags, which would have been awesome, except that envelope-style bags are kinda useless. (What do you put in there? Other envelope-style paper bags?) Flat-bottomed paper bags were a lot more useful, but they had to be folded and glued by hand, an incredibly expensive and labor-intensive affair that would require women like Margaret, now thirty years old, to sit on their butts all day folding and gluing. Realizing this inefficiency was impractical (and growing impatient with the myriad of dudes who had tried and failed to make a flat-bottomed paper bag machine), Margaret decided to fix the problem herself. Over the next two years, she worked on her design *all the dang time*. She took so much time off from her job that her manager complained (she attempted to placate him by offering to sell him the design, which fortunately he never took her up on). Finally, after tons of toil, Margaret came up with a functional wooden prototype of a flat-bottomed paper-bag manufacturing machine that did the work of *thirty* humans!

And *this* time, she was intent on patenting that sucker. The process required that she present to the patent office an iron model of her machine, something she couldn't make on her own. So she brought her design to a machine shop to have it replicated in cold, hard metal, and all would have been well had not a certain copy-cat named Charles Annan popped into the shop. Annan took one look at her machine and thought, "Hm, that seems like something I would like to pretend to have invented." He then filed a patent for it under *his* name. Margaret, understandably, was mega not cool with this preposterous plagiarism, and she took Annan to court—which wasn't cheap. Now thirty-three years old and working as much as possible in real estate (and hating it), Margaret had to shell out $100 a day (!) just to keep her Washington patent lawyer in the courtroom. Adding insult to injury: Annan's major defense of "his" invention was basically: women can't invent stuff, so no way it's hers.

Which sounds patently (heh) ridiculous to our modern ears, sure, but this was 1868. Women inventors were incredibly uncommon, yet they still managed to get blasted in almost as many think pieces by grumpy old white dudes as present-day grumpy old white dudes pen about Millennials and their cell phones. Even the texts that praised women's innovations came off pretty sexist. An 1870 *Scientific American* column proudly announced that, despite seeming incapable of "anything higher than a pound-cake or a piece of embroidery," women can actually build machines "fully equal to the same number of inventions selected at random from among those made by men." Gee, thanks. At least the *Boston Daily Globe* would acknowledge—*forty years later,* in 1909—that gals doing more than the "making over of old hats" can only happen when women are afforded "the opportunity and the inclination to so exercise their talents." No kidding.

Well, Margaret had opportunity, inclination, *and* a fightin' spirit to defend her rights, and so she gathered witnesses from around Massachusetts who could attest to her machine skills. Her former bag factory boss testified that the "idea of a machine for the manufacture of square-bottomed bags originated in conversation between Miss Knight and myself" and that he "most certainly ha[d] no doubt that it was her idea." Her mechanic said that the iron machine had been made from Margaret's wooden design. Eliza McFarland, a gal pal of Margaret's with whom she would later live for over forty years (though none of the literature on Margaret ever bothers to mention that detail—*can't imagine why*), reported that "I know what I saw. . . . I saw her making drawings continually . . . always of the machine. She has known nothing else, I think." Describing herself, Margaret said that she had, from her "earliest recollection been connected in some way with machinery" having produced a ridiculous number of papers and models documenting her design process from as far back as 1867, including entries from her personal diary that she refused to read aloud (saucy sample entry: "Heigh ho, can't see how to turn that fold back—unless . . . "). It worked: Margaret won her case, and in November 1869 she filed the necessary paperwork under "Margarett E. Knight." She was awarded a patent in 1871 and either received or refused $50,000 for it (sources differ, but still, that's a huge number).

After that, pretty much everyone was about the flat-bottomed paper bag, which was way, way better than the net bags or boxes people had until then used to carry groceries. Margaret teamed up with a rich business dude from Newton and founded the Eastern Paper Bag Co. in Hartford, Connecticut, but things were still sticky. According to an 1871 article in *Woman's Journal*, guys were "sceptical as to her mechanical ability" (read: sexist). Other factory superintendents would tell journalists that women couldn't be inventing things because they "cannot keep the machine in order. Their dress is objectionable, particularly hoops, which take up much room, and are in danger of getting in the machinery" (cool, more sexist delusions). But "by going daily, and working among them—detecting mistakes, and improving plans, with a keener eye than any man in the works," Margaret made them all change their tunes. Buoyed by some hard-earned paper-bag money bulging in her pockets, she set up a workshop in Boston and a residence in Framingham. She earned a living by retaining some interest in her patents before selling them to huge companies (like the shoe-leather cutting machine she sold to Boston Rubber).

As the times changed, so did Margaret. After two years in the hospital for an unspecified illness, she began working with cars and, in her early sixties, designed a ton of different engines and engine parts run by everything from gasoline and kerosene to acetylene. The media remained fascinated with her, too. A 1912 article praising her prowess with automobiles reported that her paper bag machine continued to be widely used and that, at age seventy-five, she was still hard at work and constantly inventing. The *New York Times* (in response to a "well-known physician" who said that "women have failed to produce works of genius, or have made any important discoveries") reported that at the age of seventy, Margaret was working twenty hours a day on her eighty-ninth invention (though only some twenty-odd were patented) and that she had received a Royal Legion of Honor from Queen Victoria. A *Washington Herald* reporter who showed up at her house for an interview "was given quite a jolt" when he discovered that "Knight" was a woman in her sixties (good pre-interview research, bud!) who preferred "to produce results rather than talk about them." The *New York Sun* reported that Margaret would respond to requests for photos of her face by supplying photos of her motors. She did once grant an interview to *Motor World* for a profile that described her as a "rather tall, strongly-built, white haired woman" who was "gentle spoken" with little desire for fame. "I suppose that it does appear odd," she told them, "that a woman should figure as an inventor of an engine; but in my case it came naturally. I was inclined that way, and have had to do with machinery almost all my life." When asked her why some men's designs at the show looked similar to hers, which she had come up with sixteen years prior, "she merely smiled, and said, 'You may draw your own inferences.'" (The *shade*!)

Sadly, not long after enduring several additional legal battles over patents (which she won) and the death of her sister in her home, Margaret again fell ill while working on her "silent Knight motor"; after a three-month struggle she passed away on October 12, 1914. Obituaries praised her as the "woman Edison" (except maybe he was the "dude Margaret"?) and "the greatest woman inventor in America." At the time, her portrait hung in the Patent Office in Washington, D.C., although her patent agent had gotten his hands on her likeness only by telling the media-shy Margaret that the portrait was for his wife's personal collection.

Today, a plaque on her cottage in Framingham identifies her (incorrectly) as the first woman awarded a U.S. patent, and her paper bag machine is in the collection of the Smithsonian Institution. But you don't have to go too far to appreciate her inventions—just swing by your local grocery store or the nearest fast-food restaurant.

Miriam
BENJAMIN

1861–
1947

AMERICAN INVENTOR AND ADVOCATE

"Be it known that I, MIRIAM E. BENJAMIN, a citizen of the United States of America, residing at Washington, in the District of Columbia, have invented certain new and useful Improvements in Gong and Signal Chairs for Hotels, Restaurants, Steamboats, Railroad-trains, &c."

Being a lady inventor is difficult, sure. But being a lady inventor of color in nineteenth-century America compounded that difficulty by a factor of a *very large number*. Fortunately for history, Miriam Benjamin was the kind of resourceful, intelligent lady who liked a challenge.

Miriam Elizabeth Benjamin had inspiring female role models right from the start. The oldest of five siblings, Miriam was born in 1861 (though she liked to say 1868, which I respect) to a Jewish dad and a Black mom. By all accounts, her mother *rocked*. Miriam's younger brother Edgar called her "the best mother that ever lived," a woman who raised her children "single-handed and alone to fight climate and privation so that her children might 'get a good schooling.'" Her maternal determination paid off: young Miriam attended elementary school in South Carolina (hardly a friendly environment for free Black women in the post–Civil War era) and then high school in Boston. By 1888, at the age of twenty-seven, she had landed teaching positions at segregated schools in Washington, D.C.

Like her mother before her, Miriam cared about education, and she was a darn good teacher to boot. For the better part of the next decade, she was continuously employed in different capacities, like "physical culture," in overcrowded schoolhouses whose conditions were unsanitary for children. But before she started bringing up the next generation of Black excellence, Miriam was coming up with ways to improve the world—a world that often told her she had no place in it, that she didn't belong, that she wasn't wanted simply because of her skin color and her desire to do more than just clean house or cook.

Miriam knew that the right technology could make the working woman's life much easier, and so on July 17, 1888, she filed a patent for a device she hoped would do just that. Her "Gong and Signal Chair" (which is not a medieval torture device or marching band instrument, even though it kind of sounds like one) was essentially a chair with a button on it that, when pressed, illuminates a light on the back of the chair. It was a *huge* thing at the time—the chair could be "used in dining-rooms, in hotels, restaurants, steamboats, railroad-trains, [and] theaters" to reduce business expenses "by decreasing the number of waiters and attendants, to add to the convenience and comfort of guests, &c., and to obviate the necessity of hand-clapping or calling aloud to obtain the services" of waitstaff. (The chair was *so* wicked awesome it may have even been adopted by none other than the U.S. House of Representatives so that members of Congress could use it to signal their pages from the floor.) Basically, it did what all great inventions do: saved people time and effort.

Even greater than that, Miriam's invention likely helped make her the second Black woman in America ever to get her own patent. I say *likely* the second (the first probably being Sarah Goode, with her 1885 folding cabinet bed) because the records aren't totally clear. Inventors didn't have to disclose race on patent applications, and it was only sometimes noted in legal documents attached to the invention or attendant court cases. Adding to the confusion is that women of color would either pass as white or submit their inventions under the name of a white man to make sure they won approval (and not be rejected for the reason of "People in Power Being Bigots"). In any case, Miriam had accomplished something very few ladies of color had done in the United States at that time, and everyone was taking note. The *Iowa State Bystander* (a Black-run paper) reported that Miriam's invention "is being commented upon by many Caucasian journals. The publishers seem to think it a phenomenon that a colored woman obtains so popular a patent. This is another proof on the list that some Negro is sure to do everything that anyone else has ever done. Their aspirations are as high as any other race."

With success tucked into the pocket of her sensible-yet-stylish dress (she did not mess around), Miriam took the opportunity to explore other career options available to her; she casually tried out medical school and possibly even law school at Howard University before looking for employment. Having passed the civil service examination with "very credible" high percentages in July 1884, Miriam got a job as a government clerk, where she did everything from folding in the printing office, to assisting in the Census Office, to helping people solicit patents to achieve the same success she'd had at such a young age. She's even listed as the attorney on her brother Lyle's 1893 patent for a device "to keep the broom moist while sweeping without being so wet as to drip, and to prevent the dust from rising." (Did he just invent the Swiffer? Sounds like it.)

Amazingly, Miriam wasn't about just helping people through her inventions and her teaching and her government work and, you know, her general incredibleness. She was also about helping those in need when it mattered, no matter how long it took. In May 1906 the *Boston Globe* reported that "through the untiring efforts of Miss Miriam E. Benjamin of Boston, a clerk in one of the departments at Washington, $10,482[.80] has been awarded to Samuel Lee, a negro who was elected to congress twenty-five years ago, but never sworn in." That's right—in 1880 a Black man named Samuel Lee had run for Congress against a white incumbent, J. R. Richardson, in South Carolina, won by 284 votes, and was promptly not sworn in and never paid. Miriam, in Washington, had heard the story by word of mouth and tracked down Samuel (who was by then quite ill). "The government should pay you," she said, according to the *Globe.* "I don't believe it will stand for Richardson receiving the salary, while you were legally elected and entitled to the same. I will try to get you the money." With the help of her brother Edgar— now a highly successful lawyer in Boston—she took Samuel's case all the way to the Appropriations Committee in Washington, where a bill was framed that would necessitate Samuel's restitution, and after a years-long fight in the House, it finally passed in 1906. Despite harsh opposition from a representative from Illinois, the then-deceased Samuel's estate was awarded over ten grand for two years' back pay (that's nearly three hundred thousand bucks, today), giving his kids what "their father should have received had he been seated as he should have been, as the vote showed." And all thanks to the relentless brigade of our gal Miriam.

Miriam went on inventing even while helping others, coming up with nifty new gadgets such as a pinking device for dressmaking. Sadly, she was struck with frequent bouts of ill health, and in 1909 she suffered debilitating back injuries after the train she was riding hit a car (she sued, natch). Forever a family-minded gal, Miriam lived out the rest of her life unmarried in Boston, in the company of her sweet mom and her cool bro Edgar (who also did a little tinkering and invented something called a "Trouser Shield," the use of which I'll leave to your imagination), until her death in 1947. Today we can remember her every time we stand up for what's right *and* every time we press that button over an airplane seat to flag down an attendant for an extra bag of delicious pretzels. Ding-dong, babes: gong and signals forever, and inventions and justice for all.

Bessie Blount
GRIFFIN

1914–
2009

AMERICAN NURSE AND INVENTOR

A woman who comes from a seriously hardscrabble background yet still dedicates her life to helping the less fortunate is probably one of the most beautiful things in the world. Bessie Blount was one of those ladies and then some, and someone should build a statue in her honor in a visible and highly trafficked area.

Bessie was born in rural southeastern Virginia on November 24, 1914, to George Woodard and Mary Elizabeth Griffin, a couple who had next to nothing. Though it had been roughly half a century since slavery was outlawed in America, racism was still alive and well, and Bessie's options as a Black woman in the small town of Hickory were limited. Just like her mother, Bessie attended elementary school at a one-room schoolhouse called Diggs Chapel, a church built by Black members of the local community after the Civil War; it was meant to educate former slaves, their children, and Native Americans. Bessie and her classmates didn't have textbooks (though eventually they would receive hand-me-downs from white schools in the area), so they learned to read by quoting verses from the Bible. Discipline was harsh, and the rod was not spared. When one of Bessie's teachers swatted her on the knuckles for writing with her left hand, Bessie taught herself to write with not just her right hand, but with her feet and even her teeth. Clearly, Bessie was willing to take on any challenge while laughing in its face.

Which was a good thing, because she was about to take on a lot of 'em. After Bessie's family moved to New Jersey, she was forced out of school by the sixth grade. Undaunted, Bessie pushed hard to receive her GED in order to qualify for college, enrolling for training in both nursing (at Community Kennedy Memorial Hospital in Newark, the state's only Black-owned hospital) and physical therapy (at Union Junior College and Panzer College of Physical Education and Hygiene). By 1944 Bessie's desire to help the helpless had taken her as far as Chicago, where she studied physiotherapy and industrial design (and also a little modern dance) before heading to the Bronx. It was there that she found her first true calling.

Bessie was among the Red Cross's Gray Ladies (so called because of their snazzy gray dresses and veils) working at Veterans' Hospital Base 81, where she helped to rehabilitate World War II veterans, especially those who were disabled and trying to readapt to their lives stateside. "You're not crippled, only crippled in your mind," she would tell them, teaching them to write with their feet or their teeth, just as she had. She even set aside a room in her own home so that she could help patients more effectively. But for vets missing limbs, the challenges of mobility were greater, especially for basic tasks like eating. What new techniques or technology could be used to improve their lives?

With her background in tech, dance, and physical therapy, Bessie started to think in all directions to solve the problem. Wanting her patients to have as much agency in their lives as possible, the then-thirty-seven-year-old inventor set to work on a kind of electronic feeding tube for people who had lost limbs. She worked tirelessly (and sleeplessly), tinkering with her device between one and four most mornings. To create her invention, she used only plastic, boiling water to mold the material, a file, an ice pick, a hammer, and some dishes. The way it worked was pretty nifty: the tube would be attached to a food receptacle, which in turn was powered by a motor; every time the patient bit down on the tube, it would send a morsel of food zooming into their mouths. This allowed patients to control exactly how much to eat, and they could do so unassisted. Bing. Bang. Boom. It worked.

Bessie patented her invention and soon was hailed by the press as "the wonder woman" for her achievements in rehabilitation. The director emeritus of the American College of Surgeons even called her feeder "a most ingenious apparatus." The VA was less convinced (or less willing to spend money) and turned down Bessie's offer to sell the device to them for $100,000. No big—Bessie decided to donate her invention to the French government, which would go on to use it in military hospitals countrywide. But why would someone just *give* away such a brilliant design? "It may seem strange to be so happy over giving something that I spent five years and more than $3000 perfecting," she said, "but I did what I thought best." Bessie was less interested in personal fame, and more determined to prove "that as a black female we can do more than nurse their babies and clean their toilets."

Besides, the feeding tube wasn't Bessie's only medical invention. She also patented a "portable receptacle support" (basically a bowl that you strap around your neck to eat from) that allowed "all persons suffering from a temporary or permanent impairment of the use of the arms and hands to conveniently and in comfort drink fluid from cups or bowls supported by the device." And while acting as physical therapist to a nice older lady, she came up with a way to make a disposable emesis basin (read: bile bucket) out of baked newspaper, flour, and water—which, despite being super environmentally friendly, was yet again not good enough for the VA to purchase (but which *was* good enough for Belgium, where it's still used today). Oh, and that nice older lady Bessie assisted? She was the mother-in-law of Theodore Edison, son of Thomas Edison, whose company would go on to produce some of Bessie's devices. Inventor Inception. (*Bwaaaam.*)

Inventing wasn't Bessie's only calling, however. While she was busy improving veterans' lives and helping people with disabilities maintain their dignity, she also fought for the desegregation of state-supported institutions whose mission was the education of people with disabilities. In addition, she wrote columns for the *New Jersey Herald News* and the *Philadelphia Independent*, for which she covered everything from Fidel Castro's visit to Harlem to Lyndon Johnson's presidential nomination. And as if that workload wasn't enough, she joined the NAACP to do public relations work *and* wrote several medical papers that were published in respected journals, including one about "medical graphology," or the relationship between a person's health and their handwriting. The latter would become kind of an important thing in Bessie's life because, in 1969—sick of the VA ignoring her sweet skills—Bessie started working as a forensic scientist for the police departments of Vineland, Norfolk, and Portsmouth. She went on to master the detection of forgeries with her amazing eye for handwriting and eventually assumed the role of chief document examiner until 1972, when the state of Virginia centralized its document examination. Rejected by the FBI because of her race, Bessie jumped across the pond to the United Kingdom, where—at age sixty-three!—she became the first American woman ever accepted into advanced studies at the Document Division of Scotland Yard. (The sweet British lads even took to calling her "Mom Bessie," aww!)

But Bessie was *still* not done. For the next twenty years, she ran her own forensic science consulting business in the United States, for which she examined active court cases and historical records—that is, a ton of slavery-related papers, Civil War documents, and museum-held Native American–U.S. treaties—because she was all about helping people forever. Despite having racked up a literal lifetime's worth of inventions, Bessie refused to give any of her gadgets to museums. "Why should I donate things I made, and they'll charge students to go and see them? No!" she said. "I'll take them to schools where the kids can hold them, touch them. I tell them, 'You're a part of history.'"

And so she did. In 2007, at the age of ninety-three, Bessie boarded a bus and traveled back to her hometown of Hickory with a suitcase full of old documents to show the people of Diggs Chapel what her life had been like at the beginning of the twentieth century. She wanted to build a library and museum dedicated entirely to the preservation of the town's civil rights history, or, as she said, "a place for your children, grandchildren and future generations to come and see what it was like for slave children right after the Civil War. There's no reason these things should be lost from history."

After all that, you'd think maybe this lady might feel the effects of her many years, but nope. "A lot of people thought I was dead already," Bessie told the local paper in Hickory during her visit. "But I ain't gonna die now. I'm gonna live just for spite. 'Cause my work is not done." She worked some more, until she passed away two years later, in 2009. Despite her long and well-known legacy, Bessie's photo is often attributed to the Black inventors Marie Van Brittan Brown and Miriam Benjamin (thanks for that, Google Images, but there's actually more than one Black woman inventor). But you and I know better than to get sucked into the Internet's lies. Instead, let's get sucked in by Bessie's bravery and then get to work building a statue in her honor.

Mary Sherman MORGAN

1921–2004

AMERICAN ROCKET SCIENTIST

> *"She let her achievements speak for her. She didn't fight a public battle about whether women could or should do the work—she just did the work."*

Next time you brush off some task as easy because it's "not rocket science," think of Mary Sherman Morgan. For this amazing midcentury woman, it was *all* rocket science—and basically none of it was easy.

Born on a farmstead in rural North Dakota (so James T. Kirk!), Mary was the youngest of six children. She grew up in a family of bullying siblings and indifferent parents who kept her out of school to work on the farm until she was eight years old, when social services stepped in, threatening to arrest Mary's father unless he allowed her to leave the house. The social worker provided Mary with riding lessons and a horse that would take Mary to and from the one-room schoolhouse.

Fortunately, the late start didn't hinder Mary's passion for education. After learning how to read and write while still managing to handle all her farm chores, she focused hard on her schooling and kicked the odds in the teeth by graduating as her high school's valedictorian, despite being three years older than the rest of her graduating class because of enrolling so late. After running away from the farm to study chemistry at DeSales College in Toledo, she lodged in secret with her estranged aunt Ida. But her education would hit another bump: midway through her undergraduate years, the Second World War broke out. Among the upheaval caused by the conflict were new employment opportunities for women. As men headed off to fight, their now-vacant jobs had to be filled. Suddenly, a whole swath of the female workforce that might have otherwise been relegated to the secretarial sidelines was able to step up and apply for the openings—with Mary being among them.

Sometimes the jobs came knocking. While at college Mary had been approached by a "local employment recruiter" who needed "factory workers" trained in chemical engineering for a job in "Ohio." As you may have assumed by my prolific use of "scare quotes," the job the man presented wasn't *quite* what it seemed. In fact, the recruiter refused to say exactly what the work was, what the factory made, or where exactly it was located. Fortunately, Mary wasn't afraid of opportunity (even when "opportunity" meant "strange dudes offering sketchy jobs"), so she accepted the offer, even when she had to get "top secret" security clearance from the U.S. government in order to do so. Hoping to complete her degree later, but also needing money to eat and survive, Mary bailed on college after sophomore year and accepted the position.

As it turned out, this supposedly ordinary factory job (and "definitely not spy stuff at all") was in the Plum Brook Ordnance Works munitions factory near Sandusky, Ohio, the country's top supplier of gunpowder, producing 400,000 pounds of explosives per *day*. As an employee, Mary created chemical compounds like DNT (used for making TNT), pentolite (used for firing warheads and bazookas), nitroglycerine (a liquid explosive), and TNT (aka trinitrotoluene, aka the explosive you may recognize from many a *Looney Tunes* cartoon). An impressive worker, Mary was devastated when she discovered she was pregnant (for a Catholic working woman without a husband in the 1940s, not the best news), and she knew she was on her own when the father, her college sweetheart, dropped off the face of the Earth after she told him about their future baby. In 1944 she gave birth to a daughter, who was adopted by her cousin, Aunt Ida's daughter Ruth (married but unable to have children). To afford postnatal care, Mary worked for three weeks at the hospital with other unwed mothers.

After the war, Mary rocketed ahead (get it?), trying to stave off the unemployment that faced so many women after the war. She boarded a bus for California and applied for a job as a theoretical performance specialist with North American Aviation (NAA), an aerospace manufacturer that designed and produced rocket engines, where she would calculate how new propellants were expected to perform. Thanks in large part to the sterling recommendations she brought from Plum Brook (a highly respected institution after the war), Mary was officially hired in 1947. The NAA brought her on as an analyst—a special word for an engineer without a college degree whom they could therefore pay less money—in the Aerophysics Lab at the NAA's Canoga Park Office, later renamed "Rocketdyne." Mary was one of 900 engineers in the company, but the only one without a college degree, and definitely the only woman.

Despite seemingly insurmountable odds, Mary was named technical lead on NAA's next big contract: developing a new fuel for the Jupiter missile. (Contrary to its name, the Jupiter was not a weapon sent to kill aliens on the eponymous gas giant, but rather a standard-issue medium-range ballistic missile used for blowing up bridges and other military targets.) Mary's job was to produce a fuel that would replace the current formulation (composed of 25% water and 75% ethyl alcohol), providing a combustion powerful enough to propel a satellite all the way into space (a feat the United States had not yet accomplished). In addition, the fuel had to be stable enough not to cause the rocket to explode on the launch pad (which was happening, like, all the time). And because the rocket machinery could not be altered, Mary had to improve the propulsion by changing *only* the chemical composition of the fuel—a task that most people thought impossible but that would see Mary facing a pink slip should she fail. Faced with this formidable challenge, Mary developed a fuel made up of 60 percent unsymmetrical dimethylhydrazine ($H_2NN[CH_3]_2$) and 40 percent diethylenetriamine ($HN[CH_2CH_2NH_2]_2$). That would get mixed with liquid oxygen, or LOX. Mary, being wonderful, wanted to name her new fuel "bagel." (Because bagel . . . and LOX. Delicious!)

Unfortunately for the world of rocket-science-related puns, the U.S. Army settled on the name hydyne. Regardless of what it was called, the fuel worked! Hydyne increased thrust by 12 percent and effectively launched the United States' first satellite, *Explorer I*, into orbit on January 1, 1958. (Of course, it was *Explorer I*'s designer Wehner von Braun who was lauded as the savior of the space program amid the formation of NASA that July.)

While working toward this blast of success (get it?!), Mary married fellow NAA employee and mathematical engineer Richard Morgan, and the couple would go on to have four children (one of whom is about to become crucially important to our story—stay tuned!). Mary retired in the late 1950s from an NAA office that then boasted at least a dozen women, and pretty much never spoke of her work again. She died in 2004, her passing marked by no major praise or plaudit, even though she was one of the world's first female rocket scientists, without whom we may never have reached orbit.

Luckily for planet Earth, Mary's son George Morgan was not about to let this injustice stand. After being approached at his mother's funeral by a man who told him that Mary had "single-handedly saved America's space program . . . and nobody knows it but a handful of old men," George began digging into her past—and what he found was astonishing (as you know after reading all about it). When the *Los Angeles Times* refused to publish Mary's obituary because it was unable to verify her accomplishments, George set out to make his mom a household name: he wrote a play about her called *Rocket Girl*, which was produced and performed at the California Institute of Technology in November 2008. Not content with already being the sweetest son ever, George published a complete biography of his mother in 2013—*Rocket Girl: America's First Female Rocket Scientist* is three hundred pages celebrating the life of this fabulous but forgotten space-age heroine. He also swooped in and saved the day when an anonymous editor tried to give Mary's supervisor credit for the invention of hydyne on Wikipedia (because, let's get real, we know where people get their facts these days).

So now that we all know the truth, let's never forget Mary Sherman Morgan, the raddest rocket scientist of them all.

PERFUMERS, PROGRAMMERS AND BOARD GAMERS

Other Amazing Women of Innovation

TAPPUTI

CA. 1200 BCE History's first documented chemist (i.e., a person who uses specialized equipment and chemical processes to make new compounds) was in fact a perfumer: Tapputi-Belatekallim, a Babylonian woman who mixed up scents in ancient Mesopotamia. Cuneiform clay tablets tell us that Tapputi, an overseer at the royal palace (that's what Belatekallim means), extracted and distilled essential oils from plants using a process she developed, based on modified kitchen items and cookery recipes. Tapputi made oils and salves for the king, along the way inventing several notable distilling, extracting, and sublimating processes (as did another Mesopotamian female perfumer and author whose name has, sadly, been lost to time).

ELLEN F. EGLIN

BORN CA. 1849; ACTIVE 1888 Ellen Eglin, an African American housekeeper in Washington, D.C., invented an improved, more efficient clothes wringer for washing machines. But instead of getting rich as heck, Ellen (whose surname is sometimes incorrectly cited as Eglui) sold her invention for a mere $18 to a white agent (who then proceeded to get rich as heck). The decision was sadly pragmatic; as Ellen said in an 1891 interview, "If it was known that a Negro woman patented the invention, white ladies would not buy the wringer." Ellen began work on another device that she was determined "will be known as a black woman's." Hoping to showcase it at the Women's International Industrial Inventors Congress, she attended an inventors' reception hosted by U.S. president William Henry Harrison. We don't know what became of Ellen—or her inventions—after that.

ELIZABETH MAGIE

1866–1948 Did you know that a lady invented Monopoly? No? Well, meet Elizabeth Magie. The daughter of an Illinois abolitionist, Lizzie worked as a stenographer, a job that helped her save enough money to buy her own house and property in Washington, D.C. (pretty unusual for a woman at the time, and totally shades of things to come). In the evenings, Lizzie expressed herself creatively: writing, acting, drawing . . . and inventing a board game. In 1903, inspired by the anti-monopolist writings of the political economist Henry George, Lizzie developed and patented the Landlord's Game, "a practical demonstration of the present system of land-grabbing with all its usual outcomes and consequences." So why don't people know about her? Because Charles Darrow is credited with the invention. Darrow had played a version of Lizzie's game, copied the rules, and then sold it to Parker Brothers. He went on to make millions, while Lizzie reportedly got a measly $500.

MADAM C. J. WALKER

1867–1919 Sarah Breedlove, the first free child in an enslaved family in Louisiana, was married at age fourteen and widowed by twenty. She found work as a washerwoman in St. Louis, earning less than a dollar a day and being exposed to chemicals so strong that she began balding. Determined to provide an education for her young daughter, she soldiered on. After marrying Charles Joseph Walker, Sarah used knowledge from her brothers in the barber's trade, as well as her own brief stint as a haircare saleswoman, to develop the Madam C. J. Walker line of products to make Black hair more "manageable" (read: more like white people's hair). Problematic? Perhaps. But Madam Walker turned her product line into an empire, starting with mail order sales and building up to the salons and beauty schools that made her the first female self-made millionaire in America. She used her success to advance the rights and careers of African American women across the country through tireless work for the NAACP. Her legacy lives on in her great-great-granddaughter A'Lelia Bundles, an Emmy Award–winning news producer and Madam C. J.'s biographer.

RUTH WAKEFIELD

CA. 1903–1977 Next time you stuff a delicious chocolate chip cookie into your mouth, you can thank this darling right here (though maybe not with your mouth full). A dietician, food lecturer, and graduate of the delightfully named Framingham State Normal School Department of Household Arts in Massachusetts, Ruth bought a tourist lodge near Boston with her husband in 1930. Called the Toll House Inn because of its history as a fee-gathering rest stop for travelers, the inn became famous thanks to Ruth's cooking, especially her desserts. In 1938 she devised a new recipe on her way back from a trip to Egypt, adding a bar of Nestlé semisweet chocolate to an English biscuit-style cookie to create the first chocolate chip cookie. (No, don't believe the Internet; she didn't run out of nuts or any such nonsense. She just worked hard and was incredibly clever.) The next year, Ruth sold the rights to the recipe and the Toll House name to Nestlé for $1, though she consulted with the company (for money, and maybe unlimited chocolate) for many years after.

GRACE HOPPER

1906–1992 By age seven, Grace Hopper was already dismantling alarm clocks just to see how they worked, and she pretty much never looked back. Earning a PhD in math from Yale by the time she was twenty-eight, Grace ditched academia for a spot in the U.S. Navy Reserve as part of the WAVES program (Women Accepted for Volunteer Emergency Service). She was assigned to work at Harvard on one of the first computers, forming part of the Mark I programming staff. Over the next few years, Grace created the first compiler, a program that translates high-level programming language (like Java) into machine code for computers to read. And she didn't stop there. To make computers even more programmer friendly, Grace developed COBOL—the ubiquitous and most used programming language of all time—which uses is written words instead of numbers for maximum human accessibility. Amazing Grace, indeed.

HEDY LAMARR

1914–2000 You may know of Hedy Lamarr as one of the most iconic sirens of the silver screen, but her amazing globetrotting life took her from Vienna to London to Los Angeles, through movies, marriages, Nazis, secret communications. . .and wifi. (Didn't see that coming, did you?) After escaping her fascist arms-manufacturer husband, Hedy went all-in for a career in Hollywood. Even after becoming famous, she preferred to spend her evenings at home, where she often collaborated on inventions with the avant-garde composer George Antheil. After World War II broke out, Hedy did her part by training her sharp innovator's mind to auto-targeting torpedoes. At the time, an enemy could easily send the weapons off course by broadcasting interference at the same frequency as the signal that controlled them. Hedy thought to randomize the frequencies controlling the torpedoes, a genius idea that George helped implement with his automated player piano. The technology not only worked for torpedoes, but it would also later be used to develop wireless Internet. Thanks, Hedy!

Q&A WITH
ERICA BAKER

SENIOR ENGINEER, TECH EDUCATOR,
AND DIVERSITY ADVOCATE

Q: *When did you become interested in science as a career? Did anyone encourage you?*

I was in high school and was taking a zero hour (before school started for the day) "programming" class. I'd been into computers and tech, your standard dorking around with Geocities sites and such, but the class was the first time I really gave thought to computer science. I wasn't really encouraged by anyone because truly not many knew what it was. The encouragement I got was more generalized, in the form of "do your best at what makes you happy."

Q: *What were some difficulties or barriers to entry you experienced while getting into STEM, and how did you overcome them?*

Oh, the standard "you don't belong here," "are you sure you don't mean to be somewhere else," people's stereotypes and attitudes about Black people, about Black women. I overcame it by a combination of ignoring and burying the comments. To be honest, I don't recommend that to anyone, especially the burying. It'll come back to haunt you in the form of lots of therapy!

Q: *Tell us about your work at Slack.*

I spend 80 percent of my time working on build and release engineering and 20 percent of my time working on diversity advocacy, making sure we talk about the hard subjects in the diversity and inclusion discussion, so we can get to real solutions.

Q: *You're also passionate about increasing intersectional diversity efforts in tech, encouraging companies to go beyond gender in their efforts to make workplaces more inclusive (with your projects like #RealDiversityNumbers). How do you think the landscape is improving for women of color?*

Honestly I'm not sure that it's improving . . . yet. I think we're in the nascent stages of improving the tech industry for women of color and for everyone. We're at a point where people are realizing we're not doing the hard work yet. We're not saying words like *racism* or *sexism* in those hard discussions. Instead we're focusing on myths, like the hiring bar myth and the pipeline myth. I think once we get to a place where there is real accountability, where we focus on inclusion, and where we're recognizing the importance of intersectionality, we'll start to see the landscape improve dramatically.

Q: *You once blew the whistle on salary inequity at a major tech player where you worked as an engineer. What would you say to women who are afraid to speak up about similar issues for fear of retaliation?*

Ha, I feel like "blew the whistle" is such an overstatement. More accurately, I empowered people to have the data needed to engage in discussions about salary that needed to be had. There was a point where I would have told women afraid to speak up to say screw it and do it anyway, but that's a utopian view. In the real world, people have bills, people have responsibilities, people need to make sure they continue to get a paycheck. I have an incredible amount of privilege, in that I work at a company that's comfortable with me speaking up and using my voice; I recognize that's not true for everyone. So to those women I'd say, reach out to me, and I'll speak up for you.

Q: *What advice would you give young women who want to get into STEM?*

To be honest, it's going to take a while to see major change in the tech industry. There are so many attitudes that need to be adjusted, so many biases that need to be addressed. It's going to be a meat grinder for a while. So to young women, I'd say make sure this is something you really love to do, because the love for the work, the love for technology, is what will keep you in this industry when everyone and everything else is telling you to leave.

ERICA BAKER is a senior engineer at Slack Technologies and advocate for diversity and inclusion in tech, expanding access to tech education. She started her career 15 years ago doing domain administration for the University of Alaska Statewide System before becoming a Googler in 2006. At Google, her role grew from support technician to site reliability engineer. In 2015 she joined Slack, where she focuses on build and release engineering. Erica serves on the advisory boards for Atipica and Hack the Hood and is a tech mentor for Black Girls Code. Find her online at @EricaJoy and ericabaker.com.

CHAPTER FIVE

WOMEN of ADVENTURE

Not everyone is a science genius or a math whiz—those kinds of smarts are absolutely not prerequisites to joining the geeky gal party. Some brilliant ladies in history have made their mark by doing things no one had ever done before, going places no geek had ever gone, gathering materials and plants and measurements and stories no nerd had ever dared to explore. From botanists to bicyclists, these awesome adventuring women broke the mold on everything it meant to be a lady in olden times. They followed their passions, and the world is better for it.

Maria Sibylla
MERIAN

1647–
1717

GERMAN SCIENTIST, PAINTER,
AND EXPLORER

"Ever since my youth I have been engaged in the examination of insects. . . . I set aside my social life and devoted all my time to these observations and to improving my abilities in the art of painting, so that I could both draw individual specimens and paint them in lively colors."

F or me, the phrase *lady explorer* automatically conjures a colonialist image of a quiet but hardy Victorian woman floating down the Nile in a dahabeeyah while sweating delicately under a dainty (but ineffective) lace parasol. But for Anna Maria Sibylla Merian, the term meant much, much more. Maria got into the exploring business for the cold, hard science—and she was the first person ever to do it.

Centuries before our nineteenth-century English roses were heading down to Africa, and only a decade and a half after Galileo had been put on trial for claiming that the Earth revolved around the sun, Maria was born in Frankfurt, Germany. It was 1647, one year before the end of the devastating Thirty Years' War, a conflict that began with Protestant countries' desire to split from the Catholic Holy Roman Empire. The conflict ultimately devolved into powerful people arguing over who had the most power (meanwhile, approximately one-half the people in Germany died of the fighting, famine, or ye olde pesky plague). Maria was born into a guild family; her relatives on her dad's side were publishers, part of a larger craftsmen's union that controlled who got to do the crafting and how. Maria's father owned his own printing press and engraved and published his own books (he was best known for a series of illustrated journeys to the New World), but he died when Maria was just three years old. Even though her mother remarried, this time to a still-life painter, as a girl Maria was technically forbidden from officially taking on a journeyman's apprenticeship (meaning that she couldn't travel around and learn from other artists). Instead, her stepfather, brothers, and their apprentices taught her at home, and young Maria loved it.

Admittedly, she loved it a *little* differently from the rest of her family and, you know, every other painter in the known world. Back in the day, floral still-life artists would learn their craft by staying in the studio to copy other artists' paintings of isolated flowers. But Maria was into all the *other* stuff that went down around flowers in their natural habitat—particularly, bug stuff. By age thirteen, she'd begun to collect and observe an entire array of silkworms inside, and outside she'd watch caterpillars squiggle along the ground. (Later stories would attribute Maria's troubling—to her mother, anyway—love for entomology to her mom looking at a cabinet of dead bugs while pregnant, but today we know that isn't how science works. Probably.)

Maria wasn't just watching the bugs be all weird and cute. She was acting like a tiny scientist, noticing that, in time, her fuzzy friends would wrap themselves up into tiny "date pits" (her term) and then emerge as butterflies. This notion was pretty remarkable in an era when science was 100 percent certain that frogs and insects just popped right out of the ground, fully formed. (Seriously, one guy, the seventeenth-century scholar Athanasius Kircher in his book *Mundus Subterraneus*, was like, all you need to do is drop some dead flies, honey, and water on a copper plate, bake at 450 degrees or whatever, and *bam!* you'll have your very own flies. It's that easy!) Maria knew better, and she even documented the metamorphoses of caterpillars nine years before Marcello Malpighi, the man who would ultimately receive credit for the "discovery."

When she was eighteen (Old Maid status in seventeenth-century terms), Maria married her stepdad's apprentice, Johann. The couple moved to his hometown of Nuremberg and had two girls, Johanna (named for her father, because that's how you did back then) and Dorothea (named for one of Maria's best girlfriends, another lady painter in town). Maria set up a little school to teach young girls how to paint (watercolor only, since the guilds made it illegal for women to use oils) and even started applying her own designs to linens and embroideries. It was in Nuremberg, with her husband's assistance, that Maria published her first nontext three-volume book of copperplate flower still-lifes, *Neues Blumenbuch* (New Flower Book). Maria's book of flower still-lifes looked basically like everyone else's, except she occasionally added her own flair by depicting a fly or little moth flittering around the petals. Dissatisfied with maintaining the status quo and just painting a bunch of pretty flowers (and still spending a ton of time combing through her garden, the town moat, and the gardens of her wealthy lady friends for fun bug finds that she would cultivate in her workshop), the then-thirty-two-year-old citizen scientist published two more volumes of fifty plates plus text, this time describing moths, butterflies, larvae, and host plants, entitled *Der Raupen wunderbare Verwandlung und sonderbare Blumennahrung* (A Very Long German Title about How Caterpillars Marvelously Transform and Eat Weird Stuff). Even cooler, she published the text in vernacular German instead of science-y Latin, which meant lots of regular people could read her book and understand caterpillars.

But not everything was sunshine and caterpillars. For one thing, it seems as if Maria's husband was not the greatest of guys. In 1685, having briefly moved back to Frankfurt after her father's death, Maria, her mother, and her two daughters ran away from Johann and followed Maria's half-brother to a culty religious community in the northern Netherlands. These guys—the Labadists—were hardcore Protestants who believed in forsaking all sinful earthly temptation-y goodness, and they (thankfully) told Maria that her marriage was invalid because Johann wasn't a believer. Though Johann arrived and set to banging down their door (even taking up construction jobs outside the colony walls so he could drag his wife back to Nuremberg), the Labadists refused to let him in. He eventually gave up his creepy pursuit, returned to his hometown, and petitioned for a divorce. Maria went back to using her maiden name and, as far as we know, never spoke of him again . . . although other people would. One of Maria's friends later said that Maria's life with Johann was "evil and miserable," and another paper mentioned his "shameful vices," so good riddance, I say.

Even though Maria was now trying to be intensely religious, she still loved lots of material, secular stuff like bugs and art—so much so that she began to miss her pre-Labadist life and started examining frogs on the colony land on which she lived. Maria also had access to other finds from afar. The Labadists had tried to establish a South American colony in Suriname (which the English had given to the Dutch in exchange for Manhattan in 1674), and though the colony there was abandoned in 1688 (the governor was shot by his own soldiers, colonists were humiliated by pirates and made to land naked, slaves escaped en masse to live in the jungle because screw slavery, etc.), the colonists had sent some of their finds back to the Labadists in the Netherlands. Maria gazed "with wonderment [at] the beautiful creatures brought back from the East and West Indies" (e.g., incredibly colorful butterflies and moths), but she was frustrated at being limited to seeing these creatures in their dead-and-pinned-to-a-board form. Like any good scientist, she wanted to see caterpillars alive and in situ: where they came from, what plants they ate, what they looked like in their natural habitat. By contrast, every other scientist back then was content just to get some dead bugs in the mail from overseas, chop 'em up, and be like "Science'd!" Maria, who lived for the outdoors, preferred experiential knowledge gained firsthand.

After her mother passed away, Maria took her two girls and moved to Amsterdam, where things were happenin': art had flourished in the twenty years since Rembrandt's death, Antonie van Leeuwenhoek was making the first microscopes, and Maria could continue teaching art to young women and even do some work for the city's botanical garden. Her desire to see the jungle had never faded; she just had no idea how she was going to get herself there. She lacked any real connections in the government or the church to gain access to grants, and besides, they didn't just send women with no formal education or training on adventures to the New World. The money had to come from *somewhere*. So Maria up and sold more than two hundred of her own paintings, was granted a small loan from the government, and in June 1699 bought herself and her twenty-one-year-old daughter Dorothea a one-way ticket on a ship to Suriname. She was the first person ever to self-fund an independent scientific expedition (and all before Kickstarter).

Two long, seasick months later, fifty-two-year-old Maria stepped off the ship in South America and was like . . . *yikes*. The Dutch had wrested control over Suriname from England mostly because they wanted the land to produce crops like sugar and cotton for the Dutch West India Company—which, of course, meant wealthy white plantation owners heralding over land worked by enslaved labor. When Maria landed, just before the turn of the century, many such enslaved workers had escaped to live in the jungle, but most were still in captivity and were being abused by the Dutch. Maria hated the cruelty, and in her writing she called out the colonists for their reprehensible behavior. She also faced down unbearable heat and humidity, stinging ants, mosquitoes, tarantulas, snakes, leprosy, stomach worms, fevers, and horrifying storms that would cause those same ants to swarm into colonists' homes. If she wanted to leave the much-embattled sugar plantations to observe insects in the wild, she had to grab a machete and hack through the jungle. Despite having no formal training for conducting field expeditions, Maria trekked into the harsh wilderness to do what she'd traveled halfway around the world to do: examine caterpillars in their natural environment.

Seeing the insects in real life was immediately rewarding, as Maria recalled when describing the color of one as being "like polished silver overlaid with the loveliest ultramarine, green and purple, and indescribably beautiful; its beauty cannot possibly be rendered with the paint-brush." Believing that "patience is a very beneficial little herb," Maria painted on vellum coated with a white primer, which she would then slide into a paper frame attached to a page in a bound notebook; on the opposite page she wrote associated notes, including details of the insect's habitat, reproductive habits, food, if it was nocturnal or diurnal, what its chrysalis looked like, and more. She spoke to the indigenous people of Suriname to discover their uses for plants and their names for insects, which she included along with all her observations. As the first European to ever really study the rainforest, Maria made the earliest European depictions of leafcutter and army ants and provided descriptions of a type of frog called the *Pipa pipa*, which would totally send the faint-hearted screaming in the other direction: "The female carries her young on her back; her uterus runs down along her back and she catches her seeds there and they develop. When they ripen, they work their way out of the skin, creeping out one after the other as from an egg." No thank you forever.

After just twenty-one months, Maria's planned five-year journey was cut short by a bout of malaria, and she and Dorothea headed back to Amsterdam along with a Carib (or possibly Arawak) woman who likely acted as a servant to Maria and assisted with her research. Selling specimens she had collected abroad (including crocodiles, fireflies, and iguanas) and her paintings of said specimens to pay off the rest of her trip, the then-sixty-two-year-old Maria ("still very lively," according to one purchaser) spent the next years painting, assembling, writing, engraving, and publishing her two-volume *Metamorphosis insectorum Surinamensium*. The compendium—which you could buy in black-and-white or hand-painted color editions, assuming you had the ducats for it—included one hundred images of insects, plants, and even some animals of Suriname. Yet instead of cranking out boring, static still-lifes, Maria had drawn the insects full-size through their entire reproductive cycle, from caterpillar to chrysalis to moth or butterfly, always shown near the flower or plant they used as a food and life source and as part of the food chain. No one before had examined the lifecycle of insects and the way they cohabitated with nature in this way—the book was mind-blowing to both artists and scientists alike.

Though Maria was paralyzed by a stroke and died in 1717, at age seventy (which is darn good longevity for the early eighteenth century), her daughters Dorothea and Johanna published a third volume of their mother's work after her death, before Johanna left to live in Suriname permanently. In the 1800s, a bunch of scientists tried to discredit Maria, partially because they were all *ewwwww* about women doing anything that wasn't raising babies in a kitchen, and partially because they didn't like that Maria had gleaned information directly from the native women of Suriname (with whom she had spoken at length about not only the plants that controlled the women's reproductive systems, but also their plight as slaves).

Fortunately, modern science recognizes Maria's achievement of cataloguing the lifecycles of nearly two hundred species of insects—some perhaps for the first and last time, for there's no doubt that specimens from her *Transformations of the Insects of Suriname* have since gone extinct. Her paintings are so precise that today 73 percent of the creatures depicted can be identified to their genus and

66 percent to their exact species. The German word *Vogelspinne* (bird spider) probably derives from a label on one of her engravings of a large spider capturing a bird. She was the first person to show neotropical organisms in color, and she did it all with her own money and on her own time. Maria was happiest when she "set aside her social life" or "withdrew from society" and "devoted [her] self to these investigations." Not only was she darn good at it, she also set a precedent for all future adventure science people (like you, perhaps?) to emulate and look up to.

Annie Smith
PECK

1850–
1935

AMERICAN MOUNTAINEER AND SUFFRAGIST

> "A woman who has done good work in the scholastic world doesn't like to be called a good woman scholar. Call her a good scholar and let it go at that. . . . I have climbed 1,500 feet higher than any man in the United States. Don't call me a woman mountain climber."

Can you think of anything more stone-cold hard-core than climbing a mountain, using science to measure exactly how high you are in the sky, and then planting a VOTES FOR WOMEN banner on the summit? Let me introduce you to Annie Smith Peck, who did all that and more.

Even in the beginning, Annie's literal climb to the top was no metaphorical walk in the park. Though born in 1850 to a well-off family in Providence, Rhode Island—her father was a congressman and her brothers numbered a doctor, a principal, and an engineer—Annie was a lady, so options were limited. Smart as a whip, Annie grew up competitive with her brothers in both physical and intellectual activities. She decided that it was up to her to "do what one woman could to show that women had as much brains as men and could do things as well if she gave them her undivided attention" (though she did think it was "a pity that women should have been obliged to do it in order to gain for those who need to work a fair chance and equal opportunity in any line of work"). She sailed through school all the way to her graduation from a teachers' college in 1872. Afterward, she taught a bit of Latin and math (first in Rhode Island, then in Michigan) and was generally nailin' the whole independent woman thing, which was impressive for an unmarried lady in her midtwenties long before the fin de siècle.

Eventually, Annie noticed she was earning about half the salary of her brother, who was also a teacher. Thinking that a little more schooling might help her case, she applied to Brown University—the alma mater of her dad, uncles, and brothers. Alas, not only was Brown like, "Hmm, you seem to be a woman, so nope," but also her whole family categorically rebuffed the idea. Her brother tried to argue that she was too talented to be stifled by college (what?), to which Annie responded: "Dare you say that out loud? What if you applied it to a young man? Are you crazy?" (Direct quote, no joke!) Her father told her he would not fund her education, prompting Annie to point out that she would need to support herself *somehow* (she'd made up her mind years ago that she would never get married and "that it would be desirable for me to get my living in the best possible way and to set about it as any boy would do"). She further noted that he was a total hypocrite: "Why you should recommend for me a course so different from that which you pursue, or recommend to your boys is what I can see no reason for except the example of our great grandfathers and times are changing rapidly in that respect."

With no help from her family, Annie ended up earning a bachelor's (*and* a master's) degree in Greek and classical languages from the University of Michigan at Ann Arbor, which had finally opened its doors to women. Happy that the women there were a true part of the community and "far from being appendages," she taught at a few local primary schools before accepting a teaching position in Latin, elocution, and German at Purdue University, making her one of the first female professors in the United States.

Next, Annie headed for Europe, where she explored Germany and Greece and became the first woman to enroll at the American School of Classical Studies in Athens. She then returned to America to make the rounds on the lecture circuit. Although she took a gig teaching at Smith College, a women's college in western Massachusetts (after first applying to the University of Michigan, whose officials told her, "You are undoubtedly better qualified for the position than any young man we shall be likely to get. At the same time there is no chance of your getting it"), Annie frequently returned to the Continent—which is where she finally found her true passion. Apparently climbing figurative mountains in terms of women's education wasn't enough for our gal. She decided she would start climbing *actual* mountains as well.

For Annie, mountains were *it*. She started "small," with little hills ranging from 3,000 to 10,000 feet tall (!). But upon her first visit to Switzerland, she caught sight of the Matterhorn, a mountain on the Italo-Swiss border and one of the highest peaks in the Alps. "On beholding this majestic, awe-inspiring peak," she said, "I felt that I should never be happy until I, too, should scale those frowning walls which have beckoned so many upwards, a few to their own destruction." At age forty-two, she quit her teaching job to lecture about mountaineering full-time as "Miss Annie Peck" (because she wanted the world to know that she was single and lovin' it). Through her lectures, Annie raised enough funds to get all the way to the top of the Matterhorn, making her the third woman ever to do so—and the first woman to do it in pants.

Seriously! Every other woman who had climbed Matterhorn's 15,000-foot peak, including Fannie Bullock Workman (who, trust me, we will hear of again) did so in skirts. If that sounds totally ridiculous, then you're with Annie. She thought climbing in a dress was "foolish in the extreme": a waste of strength, dangerous, and "obviously absurd." Rather, Annie argued, "suitably made knickerbockers (not so scant as men's and yet not too full) are not only more comfortable but more becoming, whether to stout or slender figures. . . . It may not be necessary to add that no one should climb mountains or even hills in corsets." Keep in mind that this was 1895, the year when one Mrs. Nova, "the first female cyclist to appear on the streets of Little Rock, Ark., clad in bloomers," was arrested for indecency. But Annie was too practical for that nonsense. She hiked in stockings, knickerbockers, a wool tunic, a heavy sweater, gloves, boots, and a hood—all while toting an ice axe. People ate it up—the Singer Manufacturing Company began giving away photos of Annie in full mountain gear with the sale of every sewing machine—and Annie was playful enough to be in on her own joke, even drawing a moustache on her high-altitude mask.

With Matterhorn conquered, Annie climbed a butt-load of other mountains like it was no big deal, calling the activity "delightful and invigorating." In 1897 she headed around the world to Mexico, where she tackled Mount Orizaba and "El Popo" (Mount Popocatepetl), neither of which had ever been surmounted by a lady. But the mountains of South America held a bonus appeal for the always-competitive Annie: many peaks were still unclimbed by *anyone*, and she was driven to do "a little genuine exploration to conquer a virgin peak, to attain some height where no *man* had previously stood." She set her sights on two mountains that were widely believed to be the highest in the Western Hemisphere: first, Bolivia's Mount Sorata, which she rocked in 1904; and second, the north peak of the Peruvian Mount Huascarán, which she climbed four years later, in 1908.

If all this sounds incredibly impressive, keep in mind that we haven't even gotten to the many logistical challenges that plagued Annie throughout her career. When she took off for Mount Sorata, everything seemed hunky-dory. The *New York Tribune* reported that she was going "to take geographical, meteorological and topographical observations, and incidentally to acquire any glory that may accrue from accomplishing a great feat." But the expedition turned out to be basically the *worst* time for the now fifty-three-year-old mountaineer. She'd brought along a male geologist and two male Swiss guides (one of whom had failed that very climb before), as well as a bunch of local male porters, and they *all* screwed her over. It took the group more than a month of travel by steamer, rail, barrels (seriously), carriage, and boat just to reach the mountain, all while avoiding bubonic plague and yellow fever. Despite ascending from sea level to 14,600 feet in fewer than three days, her male companions insisted on barging onward without taking time to adjust to the altitude. Worse, Annie started to suspect that the team's geologist was perhaps not as experienced as he claimed; after peering up at Sorata from below, he remarked offhandedly, "My, it looks cold up there." (Yes? Duh??) Sure enough, on the climb up the mountain, everything fell apart: the scientist suffered from altitude sickness, one of the Swiss guides was afraid of the local porters and kept demanding an army presence, their mule driver got drunk and stopped showing up, the guides decided they were done climbing and untied themselves from Annie, placing her in mortal danger, and once the geologists bailed, the porters stopped taking orders because they didn't believe a woman was in charge. "Never before had I felt so hopeless," wrote Annie. "Heart-sick I said nothing. It was not a question of my own capabilities. I could climb, but certainly I could not carry up tents, sleeping bags, etc. To manage three men seemed beyond my power. Perhaps some of my more experienced married sisters would have done better." Fearless and ambitious Annie had to give up.

But, fortunately, not forever. Four years later, with the help of the *New York Times* and a rich woman patron, Annie went back to scale Mount Huascarán, which she figured was taller anyway (and which *Harper's* called "one of the most remarkable feats in the history of mountain-climbing." Yeah, it was!). Equipped with food, climbing irons, flannel shirts, wool stockings, hand-sewn warm underwear (so her porters would stop complaining about the cold), a rifle and revolvers, lanterns, sleeping bags, and food (including chocolate, because she was still human), Annie hired two Swiss guides, who *once again* turned out to be complete dinglehoppers. They failed the climb *five times*—which is maybe enough times to warrant giving up if you're lazy, but our Annie was like, *let's just go already*, and again started battling her way up. After finally making it most of the way to the peak, she stopped to take scientific measurements to determine the exact height of the mountain. Turns out she couldn't because she needed an extra set of hands to deflect the wind off her, and one of her two ridiculous guides had disappeared. He had run off to see the summit first, which was a *huge* betrayal since it was Annie's expedition and rights to the discovery were hers. Though she could still say she climbed Huascarán first, *technically* he saw the peak before she did. But the traitor got his comeuppance. He was so bad at mountaineering that he refused to wear thick socks and then lost his gloves on the way down and had to have several of his limbs amputated. And even though he was truly the worst, people tried to blame his foolishness on Annie's failure as a leader, just because she was a lady.

On top of all that, most of Annie's family liked the mountain-climbing thing even less than the going-to-school thing. (To wit: in a letter to her before she climbed the Matterhorn, they wrote, "If you are determined to commit suicide, why not come home and do so in a quiet, lady-like manner." Rude.) Though her brothers supported her in theory, they didn't back up their support with the necessary cold hard cash, leaving Annie to fend—and fund—for herself. The lecture circuit earned her a living, but getting up a mountain safely and successfully required mega dollars for particulars like travel to the mountain, guides, scientists, equipment, porters, and a whole bunch of other climbing paraphernalia. (You don't just get to a mountain and walk up it like, Yeah, killed it. There's a lot involved.)

To get some extra money, Annie founded the Andean Exploration Society, asking $5 per member, especially from those who "should desire the recognition of woman's ability in whatever direction be disposed to encourage one who in an unusual line has already achieved large success and shown capabilities far beyond those of most men." She also cashed in on her notoriety from the lecture circuit by writing about her experiences for magazines and papers; they'd give her the sweet, sweet dollars and she'd write for them *and* put their banner on the mountain's peak. Of course, Annie was pretty scrupulous about her accounts, so her editor at the *New York World* occasionally needed to embellish the heck out of her cables (along the lines of, "We ate a picnic on El Popo with a very sweet child even though it was spitting lava and rocks! . . . And then the child *died a tragic death on the mountain*," and so on). This made for great reading, but didn't do much to help Annie in the not-looking-reckless department. It took her four years to gather enough money to attempt Huascarán because, as she said, "many regarded the scheme as foolish and unprofitable, some advised me to stay at home (I said I would if I had one), while others believe me insane, or ignorant of what I was planning and unable to carry it out; though the fact that I had, with little inconvenience, already surmounted over 18,000 feet was evidence that I had some ability in this direction."

And then there was ol' Fannie Workman. Fannie was another mountaineer who was rich as heck and fiercely protective of her "best at mountaineering" title—a title that Annie was now claiming in the press (at least partially to convince people to fund her future treks), saying that she held the record for the highest female climb, at Huascarán's 24,000-foot peak. To discredit her rival's claims, Fannie spent $13,000 (over four times Annie's totals) to have a group of scientists re-create the Huascarán climb and measure the mountain's height (correctly) at 21,800 feet. That was significantly less than the 23,263-foot peak of Nun Kun Pinnacle, in the Himalayas, which Fannie had surmounted two years before Annie's climb of Huascarán. (Fannie also said a bunch of really rude things about Annie in the press, which is simply inexcusable. Women should support other women!) In fact, Nun Kun measures 22,735 feet, so Fannie fudged her own records, too.

Luckily, Annie never let any of this nonsense get her down. She kept climbing as long as she could, scaling Peru's highest volcano at age sixty-five and firmly planting a Joan of Arc Suffrage League banner at the peak. She scienced hard on every mountain, carrying mercurial barometers to measure height from atmospheric pressure; hypsometers for determining at what temperature water boiled along the way; psychometers to measure humidity; thermometers to keep track of body temperature; sphygmographs to keep track of their pulses, and a sphygmomanometer to record blood pressure. (*Phew.*) She even designed special oxygen bags for climbing, though they didn't quite work.

Annie kept climbing until she was eighty-two years old, at which point one of Huascarán's peaks had been named for her, and she had received a ton of titles and awards from the Peruvian and Chilean governments for her help increasing tourism and trade to South America, through her later trips to the region by plane. (Even Amelia Earhart was an Annie Smith Peck fangirl and would go on to describe herself as "only following in the footsteps of one who pioneered when it was brave just to put on the bloomers necessary for mountain climbing.") Annie wrote several successful books about her travels (which included such hardcore quotations as "I had dangled over a precipice where the landing place was 5,000 feet below; but that was of no consequence"), lived out of a hotel and told the press her home was "where my trunk is," and was a self-avowed "firm believer in the equality of the sexes." Even though she was (and still is) a killer role model, she knew that "no woman can represent all women any more than one man represents all men."

In short, Annie Smith Peck did what she wanted, and she did it all without anybody's help, which makes her the pinnacle of awesome.

Ynes
MEXIA

1870–
1938

MEXICAN AMERICAN BOTANIST
AND EXPLORER

L ots of accomplished women get their geek on early in life—but not all. Sometimes it takes a while to get going, or get inspired, or just get out of a cruddy situation. So lest you think that you have to be a spring chicken (whatever that means) to make a difference in this world, meet the daring adventuress Ynes Enriquetta Julietta Mexia, a plant-loving lady who didn't start doing her thing until after she'd been alive for half a century.

Which isn't to say the beginning of her life wasn't interesting. Ynes was born in the Georgetown area of Washington, D.C., in 1870 to Sarah Wilmer, an American woman, and General Enrique Mexia, a Mexican diplomat who also happened to be a philanderer with more than ten illegitimate children. After moving to Enrique's family lands in Texas with her mother (who already had six children from a previous marriage), Ynes traveled far and wide for her education, attending excellent schools in Philadelphia and Ontario before finishing at St. Joseph's Academy in Maryland. With her schooling complete, she moved to Mexico City to care for her ailing father in his large hacienda. After his death in 1896, Ynes married Herman Laue, only to be faced with her husband's death a mere seven years later—years that she spent mostly defending her estate from illegitimate half-brothers.

But Ynes was intelligent and resourceful, and though the men in her life kept dying and the violent Mexican Revolution (which would claim the lives of some 1.5 million people) was right around the corner, she managed to set up a successful poultry and pet stock-raising business out of the hacienda. Ynes's hustle must have been attractive because, in 1908, she married the much younger Augustin A. de Reygados—he was twenty-two and she was thirty-eight. But before you're all "Get it, girl!" bear in mind that twenty-two-year-old males do not always make super-mature husbands, regardless of how attractive their youth may make them. Sure enough, while Ynes was in San Francisco being treated for a medical problem, Augustin managed to bankrupt her entire business. Even worse, revolutionaries were coming for her hacienda. Purposeless and penniless, Ynes ended up selling the estate for $25 an acre and, with the help and advice of her doctor, divorced ol' money-wastin' Augustin and set up a new home in San Francisco. It was a good idea, but a tough change: Ynes had faced a lot of loss in her relatively short life, and as a result she suffered a mental breakdown. She spent the better part of the next two decades in San Francisco working as a social worker while slowly recovering from her persistent feelings of worthlessness and emotional instability. As part of her recuperation, she began taking long hikes and nature walks with the Sierra Club—and that's when Ynes realized, *Holy fungi, I freaking love plants.*

And so in 1921, fifty-one-year-old Ynes enrolled at the University of California, Berkeley to take classes in natural science and botany. Though she never graduated, Ynes made connections in the California botany circles and—after completing a course on flowering plants at the Hopkins Marine Station in 1925—headed out with the Stanford botanist Roxana "Roxy" Ferris on a two-month expedition to Mexico. Ynes's knowledge of both Spanish and the Mexican countryside proved invaluable, and despite minor setbacks (like, you know, falling off a cliff and fracturing a few ribs) the two women returned to California with more than five hundred specimens, including a few plants previously undiscovered by scientists. One such example—*Mimosa mexiae*—would eventually bear Ynes's name, leaving her satisfied in knowing that there would be "permanent exhibits under my name in the Herbaria of the world for all time to come."

Discovering her purpose helped Ynes with even more than her depression. It helped her get in shape and gave her the courage to travel (alone as a woman in the 1920s) to the most obscure, remote parts of Mexico and South America. She basically became the lady Indiana Jones, only with less face melting and more plant collecting. Carrying seventy-five pounds of paper, a camera, and a typewriter, all used for drying and cataloguing specimens, Ynes traveled by train, boat, raft, mule, and even on foot into the jungle, where she followed indigenous guides called *mozos* and faced wild animals, harsh weather, and all kinds of other hardships—which sounds intense and scary, except that she loved (almost) every minute of it. In 1926 she returned to Mexico alone, rolling back into California twelve months later with thirty thousand specimens, fifty of which were previously unknown species, and even one brand-new genus of globelike flowers in the sunflower family, subsequently the *Mexianthus*, which she discovered up a forest trail in the volcanic mountains near Puerto Vallarta.

Yet because she felt she was more "a nature lover and a bit of an adventuress" than a scientist, Ynes enlisted the UC Berkeley herbology student Nina Floy Bracelin ("Bracie," for short), whom she'd met at a "Six Trips Afield" extension course, to help beef up her lab skills. Ynes convinced her friend to assist her on the sly by curating samples that Ynes returned with and helping sell them to collectors, museums (like Chicago's Field Museum), or universities (like Harvard's Gray Herbarium and the University of Michigan at Ann Arbor's Botanical Garden). Thanks to Berkeley and Bracie (who soon after was hired as an official herbarium assistant), Ynes was able to fund the rest of her adventures through the sales of her specimens. With this sweet cash money (and a good pair of pants), Ynes ventured out on treks to Alaska's Mount McKinley in 1928 (which she hated but during which she still managed to collect 6,100 specimens), Argentina, Chile, Peru and the Straits of Magellan, Brazil, and more, until 1938.

How do we know all this? Ynes wrote down lots about her adventures and published her accounts in the California Botanical Society journal and Sierra Club Bulletin. Here's a taste of her adventures: in "Three Thousand Miles Up the Amazon," she describes paddling a dugout canoe through the five-mile-long Pongo de Manseriche gorge, where Ynes and her guides were surrounded by two-thousand-foot cliff walls on either side—sometimes no more than one hundred feet apart. "From there on," she wrote, "there was no sight of human beings—only the shining, shimmering, cream-brown river, stretching from sunrise to sunset, confined by living green walls on the right and on the left, and above all the high-arched sky, delicately clouded at dawn, its intense blue relieved as the sun rose higher by fleecy white clouds, which soon piled aloft in huge cumuli, and turning black and threatening as they tore down upon us in a torrent of blinding rain, with thunder and lightning, for the afternoon storm."

Ynes describes resorting to consuming toucans, monkeys, and parrots ("I can assure you, they are not bad eating") and undertaking a dicey return trip home. Apparently the river was too high to go back the way they had come by canoe, so her company strapped some balsa into a raft, loaded it up with her plant, bird, and insect collections (and one of her guides' newly acquired baby monkey), and sailed it down the rapids, getting caught in a whirlpool along the way ("the most delightful mode of transportation I have encountered"). In "Camping on the Equator," she wrote about her 1934 journey to Ecuador for the U.S. Department of Agriculture to collect a genus of flowering plant called cinchona (known for its quinine), several types of soil-binding herbs, and a rare type of wax palm that grew in climates higher and colder than any other such tree. She took charge of the expedition, clambering down perilous trails and across bogs, pushing her (always male) guides through dangerous conditions, camping in horrible weather, poking fun at her own weaknesses, and generally having no time for anyone's crap. "In the chill, overcast morning, [one guide] complained that he had slept under a drip all night, but I did not care; why didn't he get up and fix it?" Good question.

Despite the bugs and the mountain lions and the other things she amicably described as "animated nature," Ynes maintained a cheery (if no-nonsense) disposition throughout her trips, continuing to take similar expeditions until the age of sixty-five. Her talent for amassing specimens was unmatched, thanks in no small part to her amazing ability to remember every plant she had ever seen (and therefore to determine which ones she hadn't). On July 12, 1938, just a few short months after a final trip to Mexico, Ynes died of lung cancer in Berkeley, California. The botanist T. Harper Goodspeed remembered her as "a remarkable woman . . . the true explorer type and happiest when independent and far from civilization." In the decade she spent adventuring, Ynes collected somewhere as many as 150,000 specimens. She was basically the baddest botanist who ever lived, and a late bloomer to boot.

Annie
LONDONDERRY

ca.
1870–
1947

AMERICAN CYCLIST AND JOURNALIST

> *"I am a journalist and 'a new woman,'*
> *if that term means that I believe I can*
> *do anything that any man can do."*

You've probably heard the refrain "Behind every great man, there's a great woman." Except *nope,* because that cutesy phrase only serves to reinforce the historically dominant notion that women should not draw attention to themselves; instead, they should stay on the sidelines, supporting men, never causing a fuss and *never* showing their ankles. There's nothing wrong with a woman who chooses to stay at home and be a great supporter of her family, so long as that is her choice. Sadly, however, for most of history, women were denied any other options, a fact that didn't sit right with one Annie Londonderry. Whether the world was ready for it or not, she was going to roll her way into women's rights on a revolutionary invention that was shaking up society: the bicycle.

When Annie found her way to fame in the 1890s, women's rights were politically taking center stage at long last, and it was thanks in no small part to the humble bicycle. Seriously! In 1896 Susan B. Anthony told the *New York World*'s Nellie Bly (a journalist famous for her journey around the globe) that the bicycle had "done more to emancipate women than anything else in the world." It was an international symbol of the "New Woman," a lady who (like the male "dandy") pushed back against Victorian ideals. New Women wore keys around their necks to symbolize their ownership of property; they smoked, gambled, and took jobs to obtain financial independence; they even wore bloomers or divided skirts so it'd be easier to ride—you guessed it—their bicycles. An 1894 periodical said the bicycle "fills a much-needed want for women in any station of life," for it let women at the fin de siècle get the heck out of the house and go wherever they wanted without asking for men's permission or their money. In *Wheel within a Wheel*, Women's Christian Temperance Union president Frances Willard (who learned to ride a bike at age fifty-three) called her two-wheeled ride a "new implement of power" that helped her escape the long skirts that tripped her up while walking. "I rejoice every time I see a woman ride by on a wheel," Susan B. told Nellie. "It gives her a feeling of self-reliance and independence the moment she takes her seat; and away she goes, the picture of untrammeled womanhood."

But of course, the New Woman and her two-wheeled getaway mobile were not without their share of controversy. Political cartoons, especially those in *Punch!* magazine, portrayed the New Woman as boring, ugly, masculine, man-hating brow-beaters (kind of like the way feminists get smeared by conservative media today). Pundits (i.e., men) feared the bike was sexually stimulating for women, or that it might cause them adverse health issues (keep in mind that this was a time when some people thought traveling twenty kilometers per hour on a train would give you a degenerative nervous illness, so . . .). The bloomers that made riding easier were "outrageous" and an "abomination," and women were arrested for wearing them in the streets (remember Mrs. Nova?). Some men even formed groups that threatened to stop communicating with any woman who wore such clothing (to which the ladies were probably like, Good, see ya).

Both Susan B. and Elizabeth Cady Stanton pushed back (basically "Can I live?"), and the *Chicago Daily News* scathingly rebutted the jerks in an 1894 article titled "Woman and Her Bicycle":

> *When woman wants to learn anything or do anything*
> *useful or even have any fun there is always someone*
> *to solemnly warn her that it is her duty to keep well.*
> *Meanwhile in many states she can work in factories*
> *ten hours a day, she can stand behind counters in bad-*
> *ly ventilated stores from 8 o'clock to 6, she can bend*
> *over the sewing machine for about 5 cents an hour and*
> *no one cares enough to protest. But when these same*
> *women, condemned to sedentary lives indoors, find*
> *a cheap and delightful way of getting the fresh air and*
> *exercise they need so sorely there is a great hue and cry*
> *about their physical welfare.*

Snap.

All of which brings us back to Annie. Born to a Jewish family in Latvia as Annie Cohen, in 1875, at age four or five, she immigrated with her family to America. The Cohens settled in Boston, a city plagued by anti-Semitism, and lived in a tiny tenement in one of the most ethnically mixed neighborhoods in America. By age eighteen, Annie was selling advertisements to newspapers and had married a devout Jewish man named Max Kopchovsky; she had her first baby nine months later, and two more by 1892. By the time she would decide she was ready for change, Annie would have a trio of children ages five, three, and two. She admitted that she "didn't want to spend my life at home with a baby under my apron every year." And so, determined to escape her dull life and a firm believer in woman's suffrage, Annie concocted a plan. By capitalizing on the world's concurrent obsessions with Jules Verne–inspired "'round the world" adventures, bicycling, and the battle for equal rights, she would have her escape.

On June 25, 1894, at just twenty-three years old, Annie marched in front of the Massachusetts statehouse with a group of prominent women's rights activists. After an introductory speech about how "women should have the same chances as men," the activists told everyone about an offer Annie had received from two wealthy Boston businessmen: if she could bike her way around the world in fifteen months, as the cyclist Thomas Stevens had done in the 1880s, she would receive $10,000 from them—provided, of course, that she didn't accept a single dollar of charity on the road *and* earned $5,000 to support herself before returning.

It was a pretty awesome challenge—and a great reward—except that *none of it was true*. Annie likely invented the story of the wager in order to drum up press for her trip, and it totally worked. People were excited, and Annie capitalized on that enthusiasm: she offered to sell parts of both her body and her bike for ad dollars, and people took the bait. The Londonderry Lithia Spring Water Company gave her $100 to go by "Annie Londonderry" instead of "Annie Kopchovsky." (And this in a world where female sports stars and women with endorsement deals were unheard of!)

With sponsorship in hand, the plan was set: her husband and young children gave her their support (her brother, despite being in the crowd of five hundred, didn't even say goodbye) and the *New York World* called her trip "the most extraordinary journey ever undertaken by a woman."

That is, it would be extraordinary *if* she could pull it off. Annie had never ridden a bike her in life, except a couple of times the day before announcing the so-called wager, and at five-foot-three she weighed no more than a hundred pounds. Her Columbia women's bicycle was a hefty forty-two pounds, and even though she packed only a fresh pair of underwear and a pearl-handled revolver, she was encumbered on the ride by her skirts and constricting tops. The bike paths were rocky and sandy and often far from civilization; she was limited to a speed of about ten miles per hour, and she had absolutely no muscle or tolerance for this kind of exercise, especially when some days saw her eating only an apple and sleeping under a bridge. After starting with a nine-hour day in June, it took her until September just to make it from Boston to Chicago via New York (where she stayed for almost a month with friends). By the time she did reach Chicago, she had lost twenty pounds. The *New York Times* reported that she was giving up.

In fact, it was in Chicago that Annie became determined to shrug off the social constraints assigned to her. She bought a twenty-one-pound men's Sterling bicycle and completely remade her cycling costume, throwing away the loose-skirted bloomers and throwing on a much more streamlined pair of leggings, a sweater, and a cap. Annie would say later, "I firmly believe that if I had worn skirts I should not have been able to make the trip," for her heavy bloomers were "torture" and "ridiculous." Instead, her neat knickerbockers and leggings allowed for much better freedom of movement . . . and led to two hundred marriage proposals, if her account is to be believed (and why *wouldn't* you believe that, really). With kickin' new duds, she left Chicago newly inspired, but with only eleven months to go and lots of that $5,000 left to earn.

Fortunately, Annie was amazingly good at getting the Victorian public to crack open their pocketbooks. After heading all the way back to New York, she hopped on a boat bound for Le Havre, France, where she promptly charmed the bloomers off everyone and set to work earning that five grand. She sold signed photos of herself, organized meet-and-greets, put her name on positive product testimonials, presented lectures to sold out halls through which she would pedal to wild applause, and even sold off her clothing and bicycle for advertisements: $400 bought space on her left boob, $100 for her right bloomer. The American press wasn't sure what to make of Annie: the *Buffalo Express* was impressed with her ingenuity, but the *Pittsburgh Chronicle-Telegraph* called it "degrading." Nevertheless, she had been an absolute delight in France, where one local paper announced that she had "captured the hearts of the people."

Make no mistake, Annie was a master of the well-crafted public image. In one of her stories, she describes putting her "revolver against the head of the man" in a gang of three who jumped her from behind some trees; another story finds her hunting tigers with German royalty; yet another sees her languishing in a jail cell in China after falling in the ice and taking a bullet in the shoulder amid the Sino-Japanese War. There, "while thus imprisoned[,] a Japanese soldier dragged a Chinese prisoner up to my cell and killed him before my eyes, drinking his blood while the muscles were yet quivering" (which, since this is not *Attack on Titan*, is 100 percent clearly not the truth). To different papers, Annie would say that she was unmarried; that she had studied medicine for two years and was a master of the cultivation of physical beauty; that she had a degree in law or accounting; that she was an orphan heiress; that she was related to a congressman and then, later, a senator. She told one San Francisco paper that she made it to China from India by bike, and to another she claimed that her transportation there was via steamer. She knew exactly how to play each crowd like a fiddle, and her hustle would put most modern publicists to shame.

By the end of January 1895, Annie had made it from Paris to Marseille, leaving just eight months to get back to Chicago. She promptly jumped on a *paquebot* (a French mail boat) through the Mediterranean and made some short bike jaunts across Jerusalem and Yemen before heading for Colombo and Singapore, where the *Straits Times* was kind enough to describe her as a "short woman, with a not unpleasant face." (The *El Paso Daily Herald* also said that "any horrid man who says she is not good looking ought to be taken out back of a cow shed and knocked in the head with an axe," which, wow, okay.) From there she cycled through to Saigon, Port Arthur, Wei-Hei-Wei Harbor, and Yokohama while in the company of missionaries and war reporters. She arrived back in San Francisco on March 23, 1895, two months after she'd left France, with what the *San Francisco Chronicle* called "a degree of self-assurance somewhat unusual to her sex."

But self-assurance can take you only so far, and the end of Annie's journey was the most difficult. Already drained from all that pedaling, she was injured by a horse and buggy just outside San Francisco (though not badly, despite her telling the *Chronicle* that she coughed up blood for two days). The terrain was extremely challenging, too: biking next to the Southern Pacific Railway tracks across the punishing and still somewhat unsettled American South meant carrying her damaged bicycle, riding trains to avoid impenetrable muddy roads, and even breaking her wrist when colliding with a bunch of pigs. But Annie accomplished her goal, finally arriving back in Boston on September 24, fifteen months after her initial departure, just like she'd promised. As the world watched, Annie proved that women were just as capable as men. She was a living symbol of the New Woman.

World famous, $10,000 richer (possibly), forty pounds of muscle heavier, and no longer content to live nameless in a tenement, Annie moved her family to New York City, where under the byline "The New Woman," she wrote a series of features for the *New York World*. Her first story (under the byline "Nellie Bly, Jr.," in homage to her globetrotting predecessor) told the tale of her journey through "all parts of the globe in her bloomers."

Amazingly, by her death in 1947 Annie had faded from popular memory. Only in the last decade did a distant nephew dig up her life's history and set to work winning her modern recognition. His biography of Annie was published in 2007, finally making her story available to the world for the rest of time, just as Annie would have wanted.

Bessie
COLEMAN

1892–
1926

AMERICAN AVIATRIX

"I made up my mind to try;
I tried and was successful."

The world did not believe in Bessie Coleman. White Americans never thought that Black people could become pilots. Many men—heck, even Bessie's own brother—told her that women couldn't, either. But Bessie believed in herself, and she went out and did her country proud anyway. So if anyone tries to tell you that you can't do something because of who you are, just think back to this amazing, brave, high-flying lady.

Bessie was born in the tiny settlers' town of Atlanta, Texas, on January 26, 1892—one of thirteen children born to Susan, likely a former slave, and George, who was three-quarters Cherokee. Times were hard; just because the Civil War had ended almost thirty years ago didn't mean that things were all freedom and privilege for Black people in the American South. Neither of Bessie's parents could read or write. More than a hundred lynchings took place in the South annually, and anything from "this Black person got gainful employment" to "this Black person tried to defend their property from gangs" could spur a violent mob. Because of racist poll taxes and literacy tests, Black Americans were unable to vote or have representation in the government. Jim Crow segregation meant that Black people were forbidden from riding in the same rail cars, attending the same schools, or using the same water fountains as white people.

With more and more of their land and rights stripped away every year, Native Americans in Texas weren't exactly having a great postwar life, either. Add to this dismal situation the depression that struck the nation in 1893, and things were kind of garbage for anyone who wasn't a rich white dude in the South.

Despite this challenging climate, Bessie's dad managed to get his hands on a quarter of an acre for $25 in a Black area of Waxahachie, Texas. Two-year-old Bessie's family moved into a small, three-room shotgun home and joined the town's booming cotton industry. But then George decided he was not about that racist Texas life, and he left for the Oklahoma-adjacent Indian Territory, where he would encounter less discrimination. Susan and the family stayed behind in Texas, which meant that Bessie, on top of her four-mile walk to a segregated one-room school overseen by an underqualified teacher, now took responsibility for her three younger sisters while her mom worked as maid and cook for a local white family.

Though it's easy to be like, "Yeah, that's rough, but I do my own laundry, too," let's not forget that Bessie was doing all this work with no electricity or running water, which meant lots of hefting heavy water buckets, labor-intensive scrubbing, and babies screaming by candlelight—all while Bessie was nine years old. In addition, every summer the annual cotton harvest interrupted her schooling, a disruption that Bessie hated (she was really good at math, for one thing). The budding girl genius would much rather be at home, reading aloud to her fam from *Uncle Tom's Cabin* or nonfiction books about Harriet Tubman that her mother picked up at the traveling cart library.

By age eighteen, Bessie felt a drive to "amount to something," which prompted her to save enough money to enroll as "Elizabeth" at the Colored Agricultural and Normal University, located in a Black municipality in Langston, Oklahoma. After cash ran out during her first semester, however, she was forced to head back to

Waxahachie—with the university band in tow, lauding her arrival as though she was about to play in the Rose Bowl. (Another good moral: next time you want to make the best out of a bad situation, just get a marching band to tail you wherever you go.)

By 1915, after years of humiliating and painful work as a town laundress (for which she was forced to leave clothes on her white clients' back steps to avoid being seen), twenty-three-year-old Bessie was ready for change. She bought a ticket to Chicago, climbed aboard the cramped, uncomfortable rail car designated for Black women, and made the twenty-hour trip, arriving in the city and moving in with her two brothers—Walter, a Pullman train porter, and Johnny, technically unemployed but probably funemployed by the mob, if you know what I mean. The three of them lived in the city's South Side, home to 90 percent of Chicago's Black population (a population that doubled in the decade between 1910 and 1920) and where all classes mixed together in relative peace and harmony. Since she hated what she perceived as the degrading nature of domestic service, Bessie enrolled in beauty school to become a manicurist and set up shop at a barber's on "The Stroll" (eight blocks of radness that was basically the Black Wall Street and Broadway combined). Soon she was giving perfect pedis to Chi-town's Black elite; she even won a contest for Black Chicago's fastest and best manicurist.

But Bessie wouldn't be buffing and polishing for long. Shortly after her move to Chicago, Johnny, who was a veteran, happened to mention to his sister that he thought French women were superior to American women because the former "could even fly airplanes." Instead of merely pointing out his flawed logic, Bessie decided to go ahead and prove him wrong by attempting to enroll at every flight school in the country.

I say "attempted" because—surprise!—American flight schools were not okay with a woman, let alone a Black woman, becoming a pilot. The friendly skies of the United States were anything but for a woman like Bessie, and life on the ground in Chicago was no picture of perfection either, thanks to brewing race riots. Luckily, Bessie had met a lot of influential folks at her manicure table and the Stroll's nighttime hotspots—including her mysterious husband, Claude Glenn, a man fourteen years her senior whom she had quietly wed in 1917 but likely never lived with (and then basically never spoke of again—safe to say they separated). Deciding that she would train in France, just like the pilots her brother was so all about, Bessie used her social smarts and some serious pluck to secure funding from one Robert Abbott (editor and founder of the *Chicago Defender*, a weekly newspaper read by 500,000 people) and Jesse Binga (a bank owner and real estate mogul who made his fortune by selling homes in rich white neighborhoods to Black families at a discount, then buying up the rest of the homes in the area as white residents fled). She started managing a chili joint and taking night classes in French and filled out a passport application (on which she said she was an unmarried manicurist). Then, on November 20, 1920, twenty-eight-year-old Bessie headed to Paris on her own.

In France, Bessie was *on it*. For instruction at the Ecole d'Aviation des Frères Caudon at Le Crotoy, she walked the nine miles to the airfield each day. She flew in an unstable Nieuport Type 82 biplane and once watched a classmate die in training. Her course was supposed to take ten months, but she finished in just seven; after nailing the final test of a figure-eight and an exact landing, she earned her pilot's license on June 15, 1921 (two years before Amelia Earhart!). Bessie Coleman was officially the world's first Black aviatrix.

The next September, she sailed back to New York, where the Harlem Renaissance was in full swing and the Black media were all about her. The brush with fame was great (and probably felt incredibly validating in a "told ya so, bro" kind of way), but standing ovations when she attended musicals wouldn't pay the bills. Commercial flights weren't really a thing yet (keep in mind this is only about twenty years after the Wright Brothers), so she was unable to earn money that way either. Besides, Bessie wanted to use her powers for good, not just for cash; her ultimate goal was to teach Black kids about airplanes and "make Uncle Tom's cabin into a hangar by establishing a flying school."

So Bessie headed back to Europe, where she spent time in Germany and the Netherlands learning how to be a proper "barnstormer," a trick flier who did amazing (and amazingly dangerous) air stunts for crowds at airshows. She even put together her own superhero costume, complete with military jacket, high lace-up boots, a leather coat, and goggles. With her act perfected, and some sponsorship from her old friend Robert Abbott, who publicized her as "the world's greatest woman flier," she returned to the States ready to perform—and the public was definitely ready to watch. In a rare instance of the white media acknowledging the accomplishments of a Black woman, the *New York Times* covered her first airshow in New York, reporting in an article entitled "Negress Pilots Airplane" that "about 1,000 spectators, mostly negroes, saw the exhibition, which was in honor of the Fiftieth (negro) Infantry regiment, New York National Guard."

Flying World War I Curtiss JN-4 "Jenny" biplanes, Bessie went on to perform across America, including a terrifying performance in Los Angeles during which her old plane engine crapped out midflight, nosedived at three hundred feet, and left her with several broken ribs and a broken leg (she recovered from her injuries in Chicago while giving lectures). But Bessie wasn't just doing daredevil stunts; she was also campaigning for equality. On a visit to her hometown of Waxahachie, Texas, Bessie refused to fly if organizers used segregated entrances. After they agreed not to segregate the event, she directed her team to airdrop leaflets about the event onto nearby Black neighborhoods. She even took Black women on passenger flights after a Houston show, "the first time colored public of the South ha[d] been given the opportunity to fly," according to the *Houston Informer*. And on top of all that, "Queen Bess" or "Brave Bessie," as the media dubbed her, opened a beauty shop in Orlando, lectured across America to inspire Black youths to become pilots, took a job doing airborne advertisements for Coast Firestone Rubber, and toyed with the idea of a movie career—which she promptly dropped when she was cast as a stereotypical downtrodden enslaved woman. (*Billboard* called her "temperamental" and "unreliable," but you know she was just taking a stand against racist garbage.)

A tale as rad as Bessie's had to come to an end eventually. At age thirty-four, when she was close to opening her own flight school, Bessie had finally saved up enough money (and gotten a little financial boost from her friends) to purchase her own Jenny. The plane was in Dallas, but at the time Bessie was in Jacksonville, so she had William Willis, her twenty-four-year-old white mechanic and sometimes-publicist, fly it over for her. The plane was super old and super trash—so much so that it needed several emergency landings during the trip to Florida. Once William arrived, Bessie's friends and family begged her not to fly, but Bessie wanted a test flight to ensure that everything was in working order. So on April 30, 1926, she and Willis took the bird up before a show for Orlando's Negro Welfare League's May Day celebration, with Willis in control so Bessie could undo her seatbelt and lean out of the plane to assess the best location for a parachute jump. But the plane was indeed busted, and after a mere twelve minutes in the air it took an unexpected dive and flip, hurling Bessie to her death thousands of feet below (she wasn't wearing a seatbelt). Shortly thereafter, Willis hit the ground in a fiery blaze and died on impact. A wrench stuck in the gearbox had caused the engine to malfunction.

It was a tragic—and perhaps foreseeable—end to a life of bravery and risk. But risk had always been part of Bessie's life as an aviatrix, and it was that kind of danger that made her job and her journey so interesting and inspiring to millions of Americans. A half century after her death, the Bessie Coleman Aviators Club for women of all races was founded in Chicago, and every year on the anniversary of her death their pilots airdrop flowers on her grave. She has a road named after her at O'Hare Airport, a Bessie Coleman Day in Chicago, and a postage stamp with her face on it. But beyond all the nifty tributes, Bessie inspired countless Black women to fight for their dreams, even when racist institutions (or rude brothers) try to stop them.

"Because of Bessie Coleman," said Lieutenant William J. Powell in 1934, "we have overcome that which was worse than racial barriers. We have overcome the barriers within ourselves and dared to dream."

TRAILBLAZERS, TRANSLATORS, AND GLOBETROTTING JOURNALISTS

Other Amazing Women of Adventure

JEANNE BARÉ

1740–1807 When it comes to the "girl dresses up as a guy to have a daring life of adventure" trope, Jeanne Baré was the real deal. Well-educated in her youth, as an adult Jeanne took on work as a housekeeper for and caregiver to the naturalist Philibert Commerçon; after his wife died, Jeanne became pregnant with his child. When asked to join Louis Antoine de Bougainville's oceanic expedition, sickly Philibert didn't want to miss out because of illness. So Jeanne dressed up as a dude and went along as his valet and assistant. The two were given private chambers to accommodate Philibert's equipment, allowing Jeanne to maintain the ruse—a ruse that saw her become the first woman to travel around the world, even if she did it in drag. When the ship reached Uruguay and Brazil, Philibert was so sick that Jeanne did much of the botany work herself. Her disguise was eventually discovered by some savvy Tahitians, but by then it was too late. Jeanne continued on with the journey, botanizin' and sailin' all 'round the world.

SACAGAWEA

1788–1812 (1884?) A member of the Agaidika tribe of the Lemhi Shoshone in Idaho, at age twelve Sacagawea was captured in battle by a rival tribe, then sold and forcibly married to a French-Canadian trapper. Her husband was the one the Captains Meriwether Lewis and William Clark would hire in 1804 as an interpreter on their exploration of the Louisiana Purchase, but it was Sacagawea and her knowledge of Shoshone that proved invaluable. As an interpreter and cultural liaison, she was brave from the start, rescuing capsized boats, bartering trade negotiations between tribes, scavenging for food—all while hefting a baby around on her back. Thanks to her instrumental role, the expedition made it across the thousands of miles from North Dakota to the Pacific Ocean. After her famous journey, Sacagawea settled in Missouri with her husband and two children, though some believe she returned to her original tribe and lived to be nearly one hundred years old. Either way, she had an amazing life and served as an inspiration to women activists in the early twentieth century as the fight for women's suffrage began.

FLORENCE DIXIE

1857–1905 Bored with life as a rich Victorian lady of leisure (because who wouldn't be?), a twenty-one-year-old British noblewoman named Florence Dixie left behind what she called "the shallow artificiality of modern existence" in 1878, when she took off for Chile, Argentina, and Brazil on a voyage with her family. After returning to England, she was so jazzed about everything she'd seen and done that she published a book about her experiences, which eventually spurred a correspondence between her and one Charles Darwin (she needed to correct him on something, obviously). Florence's book also nabbed her the ground-breaking position as war correspondent in South Africa during the first Boer War, proving women's capabilities on the field as explorers and as journalists to boot. Florence believed that men and women should wear the same clothes, be given the same opportunities for jobs and education, and have the same rights in marriage, divorce, sexuality, custody, reproduction, bodily autonomy, and inheritance. She later went on to write fiction, including *Gloriana, or the Revolution of 1900*, which imagines London in 1999 as a feminist utopia run entirely by women. If only, Florence. If only.

FLORENCE BASCOM

1862–1945 The child of a university president and a women's rights activist, Florence Bascom was destined for some ground-breaking business from the start. She had garnered three bachelor's degrees by age twenty-two, earned a master's three years after that, and became the first woman to get a PhD from Johns Hopkins by thirty-one (though in class she had to sit behind a screen so as not to disturb the male students' delicate sensibilities). Florence taught at colleges and universities across the United States before founding the Department of Geology at Bryn Mawr College, where she trained the first American women geologists. In 1894 she became the second woman ever allowed into the Geological Society of America; two years later she smashed barriers again when she was hired by the U.S. Geological Survey—first woman there, too. Her own research—on crystalline rocks in Appalachia—continues to influence geology to this day.

NELLIE BLY

1864–1922 The daughter of an Irish immigrant, Elizabeth Cochran had to drop out of boarding school as a girl because she didn't have enough money to pay room and board. Fortunately, her first success came soon after: at age sixteen, she wrote a passionate smack-down in response to a disgustingly misogynist article in the *Pittsburgh Dispatch* titled "What Girls Are Good For" (spoiler: not much, according to them). After landing a full-time job in journalism at *The World*, "Nellie" (a pseudonym, since at the time it was unseemly for women to publish their own writing) moved to New York and wrote about women's issues, even going undercover at the

Blackwell's Island Insane Asylum to report on their mistreatment of female patients. She became most famous for taking up the *Around the World in 80 Days* fad in 1889 and journeying around the globe in just seventy-two, passing through and reporting on England, France, Italy, Egypt, Sri Lanka, Malaysia, Singapore, Hong Kong, and Japan. By ship or by rail, Nellie traveled alone for nearly the entire trip and earned international renown for her voyage. She was an incredible investigative journalist (doing everything from exposing the abuse of the press in Mexico to joining a marching band), a fierce suffragette, and went on to marry a millionaire.

GRACE MARGUERITE HAY DRUMMOND-HAY

1895–1946 At just twenty years old, Liverpool-born Grace Drummond-Hay was married off to a hecka-rich seventy-four-year-old man. Kind of a bummer for a young and curious gal—except that her husband died just six years later, leaving Grace a rich (and still young) widow. A talented writer, she landed a job as a reporter for Hearst newspapers and rose to fame as the only female passenger of the first 'round-the-world zeppelin journey, which made stops in New Jersey, Germany, Tokyo, and Los Angeles. Despite her instant fame upon landing, Grace kept her ego in check and continued to work as a journalist for the rest of her life, including stints as a war correspondent in Ethiopia and China. She remained incredibly well respected right up until she died following internment in a Japanese POW camp in Manila during World War II.

AMELIA EARHART

1897–DISAPPEARED 1937 After working for several years in Toronto with the Red Cross, Amelia Earhart attended the 1919 Canadian National Exposition, where she watched a plane dive at her during a flying exhibition. The next year her father spent $10 for her to go up in a ten-minute flight with an air racer, and that's when

Amelia knew she had found her passion. She worked her butt off to afford flying lessons and her very own biplane, and in 1923 she became only the sixteenth woman to get a pilot's license from the Fédération Aéronautique Internationale (just like Bessie Coleman!). Three years later, Amelia was asked to be the log-keeper on a transatlantic flight from Newfoundland to Wales, making her the first woman to undertake that journey (which she would make again, solo, in 1932). On the ground, Amelia got real famous, real fast: she published a book, gave lectures, endorsed products, and even worked as an editor at *Cosmopolitan* before disappearing into the sunset while attempting a flight around the world in 1937. In the words of Eleanor Roosevelt: "She helped the cause of women by giving them a feeling that there was nothing they could not do."

Q&A <u>WITH</u>
MIKA MCKINNON

FIELD GEOPHYSICIST, DISASTER RESEARCHER, AND SCIENCE WRITER

Q: *When did you become interested in science as a career? Did anyone encourage you?*

Curiosity is a driving trait in my family, which probably explains why we have so many scientists and science lovers at holiday gatherings. My teachers were nearly universally fantastic, encouraging me to dive down rabbit holes of curiosity and giving positive feedback on my bizarre passion projects.

Late in high school, I spent a summer in the deserts of California coaxing a telescope with a broken clutch to track the asteroid 4 Flora. By day, my trio measured its location on glass plates we'd developed late the night before, frustrated by the limitations of our tools. I wrote clunky code to grind through calculations to use that data to determine the orbit for our lump of rock and ice. Like decades of students before me and all those since in the Summer Science Program, I was pushed to my limit and loved it. When I emerged from weeks of chronic sleep deprivation and submitted our results to a data repository, I felt a mess of joy and exhaustion, a feeling that would be all too familiar in the years ahead.

Q: *What difficulties or barriers did you experience while getting into STEM, and how did you overcome them?*

I am incredibly lucky. My family not only embraced the fundamental curiosity that drives the scientific process, they also understand the mechanics of the education system. And yet . . .

Field geophysics was like time traveling to an earlier era of outdated social norms. Sometimes I'd find ways to work around it, having an assistant repeat my instructions with his masculine voice when my crew blew off my higher timbre. Other times, I'd try to prove myself by taking the heaviest pack up the roughest trail. But as the petty problems escalated, my capacity to tolerate sexism broke. The more sexism I encountered, the more glittery pink I used to deck out my equipment, a visual rebellion. (Secondary benefit: my tools no longer walked away once wrapped in bright purple electrical tape!)

Q: *Tell us about your adventurous work in the field as a geophysicist and disaster researcher.*

Field geophysics is a blend of being MacGyver and a James Bond villain. A field geophysicist flies around in helicopters to remote terrain, landing on a pristine glacier, a rugged mountainside, or a quiet alpine meadow. And in Canada, fieldworkers all have their best bear story. Mine is the time I got into a territory war with a grizzly.

Geophysicists cut trails through dense forest, which bears clearly assume are highways just for them. One morning, I was trying to start work only to discover that a bear had decided that our injection point—where we were pouring 2400 volts of electricity into the Earth—was the perfect place to warm up.

Concerned for both data quality and crew safety, I tried to encourage the bear on its way by varying the current and voltage. No matter how I fiddled the knobs, the bear snuggled into the harsh metal pegs more firmly. The intimidating roar of a bear banger was absolutely useless. Desperate, we finally asked our helicopter pilot to buzz the line, which scared the bear into loping lazily away.

We finished up collecting data as quickly as possible, and

packed equipment to clear out and move to the next line. But for data continuity, we needed to leave behind a single thin wire as we continued the survey. Distracted by a conductive layer of graphite masking my hunt for gold, I forgot about the bear.

But the bear didn't forget about me. When I came back weeks later, survey completed, to clean up, I found the bear had left me a present. The remains of its dinner—blood, fur, and bones—were tangled in my wire. With two clips to isolate the mess, we gathered up the rest of the wire and left the bear alone for good.

Q: *You're also passionate about bringing science to the masses, educating people through your writing on sites like io9 and Gizmodo. Do you think making science more accessible online encourages more marginalized people to get into STEM fields?*

Our world is full of creative, curious people from all walks of life, and as a science communicator, I get to hunt for those stories and highlight people who challenge the cultural perception of who can do science. Communicating science in public can be exhilarating, but it can also be terrifying. Every mistake is out for everyone to see. But that also creates an opportunity where I can model the practice of science, making it more human and real to people who don't have scientists in their social circles.

But what I really love is that I'm not the only one doing this. Scientists have flocked to social media, discussing the messier side of their field observations or sharing their personal passions alongside their research results. We get to see, and participate in, chatter about highly anticipated experiments, and we engage in protracted, public peer review of results.

Q: *What advice would you give young women who want to get into STEM?*

Be curious. The heart of science is to investigate the world around you as methodically as possible, slowly unraveling fragments of the secrets that make up our universe. Find ways to increment our knowledge that tiny bit further.

Tell others about your work and who you are. We don't know if you don't say anything, and you might be holding the key we need to tell a story.

Be gentle with one another. The universe is vast, and the science is endless. We'll learn so much more if we collaborate and work together than if we let our petty human flaws dictate our actions. Be generous with giving credit; everyone should be recognized for their work.

Own up to your mistakes. Do your best to correct them and to learn from them. Then don't stress about it too much—it happens to everyone.

Go on adventures, whatever they look like to you. But most important, have fun.

MIKA MCKINNON is a geophysicist working with Natural Resources Canada and the Federal Emergency Management Agency to keep the planet from killing us all. She lurks on sets to gleefully interject truth, creating far stranger fiction, and pops up at conventions like Dragon Con to help you revel in the real science behind your favorite shows. Check out her writing in *Physics Today*, *New Scientist*, io9, and Gizmodo, and keep up with her latest adventures on Twitter @mikamckinnon.

HOW TO BECOME A WOMAN OF WONDER

Are you inspired to start following your passion and blazing your own trail like the ladies in this book? Here's a guide to amazing organizations for ladies of all ages looking to expand their horizons in science, technology, and beyond.

Science, Technology, and Engineering

girldevelopit.com

This nonprofit provides affordable, accessible software-development programs across the United States. There's probably a chapter of **GIRL DEVELOP IT** near you. Charlottesville (VA) has the Code and Coffee Study Group, Columbus (OH) has Hack Night, Fort Collins (CO) has an introduction to Git and Github, Ann Arbor (MI) has a lesson on Securing Your Website . . . and the list goes on. All totally worthwhile, full of beginners, and judgment free.

girlswhocode.com

Reshma Saujani, former deputy public advocate of New York City, founded **GIRLS WHO CODE**, which offers a wide variety of programs to help gals gain computing skills. Choose the Summer Immersion Program for seven weeks of intense training. Or if you're already a seasoned coder, volunteer to lead workshops for tomorrow's young women coders.

hackbrightacademy.com

This ten-week, women-only course will take you from beginner to software engineer—and 90 percent of the academy's graduates get job offers. Now *that* is a good investment. **HACKBRIGHT** even provides scholarships for women from traditionally marginalized backgrounds—score!

societyofwomenengineers.swe.org

In addition to organizing tons of events for girls of all ages, the **SOCIETY OF WOMEN ENGINEERS** offers scholarships for ladies thinking about pursuing engineering in college.

blackgirlscode.com

Kimberly Bryant felt culturally isolated while studying technology in college; she shared aspirations with her classmates, but not much else. To encourage more girls of color to get into fields like robotics and game design, she founded **BLACK GIRLS CODE** in 2011, and now there are classes at chapters all over America!

engineergirl.org

Part of the National Academy of Engineering, **ENGINEERGIRL** was founded with the support of a nationwide Girls Advisory Board. It provides helpful access to everything from mentors and scholarships to the opportunity to try on an engineering career for a day! Perfect for anyone who's ever wanted to build cool stuff.

girlsmakegames.how

Although 47 percent of gamers are female, women make up only 12 percent of the games industry. With programs ranging from Intro to Programming and Game Design to Audio Engineering and Board

Game Design, **GIRLS MAKE GAMES** has something for anyone who wants to get hands-on game-building experience—and improve those aforementioned dismal statistics.

robogals.org

Primarily aimed at girls up to the seventh grade, **ROBOGALS** was founded to rectify the fact that women make up only 10.9 percent of all engineers in Australia. Now Robogals has chapters across North America (at the California Institute of Technology and Columbia University) that are designed to get girls building and programming. How much fun would 10-year-old you have making your own robot?

girlsintech.org

A global nonprofit based in San Francisco, **GIRLS IN TECH** aims to make the world a better place for women interested in technology and entrepreneurship. It organizes a ton of initiatives for girls and women to "enhance their professional aspirations" (nice!), including conferences, hackathons, mentorships, even a two-month bootcamp.

Medicine

millionwomenmentors.org

Curious about getting into medicine or med sci, but no idea where to begin? Check out **MILLION WOMEN MENTORS** for a wicked cool lady in your area, living the brainiac dream. With over 200,000 mentorship pledges, it's mathematically proven to be inspiring. There's also the FabFems (fabfems.org), where the National Girls Collaborative Project lists mentors by ethnicity, if you want to chat with someone who has the same cultural background as you.

artemismedicalsociety.org

A global sisterhood of women physicians of color, the **ARTEMIS MEDICAL SOCIETY** raises awareness for healthcare in minority communities, hosts an annual conference, and even has an academy where women of color interested in becoming doctors can partner with existing Artemis members to help them succeed.

mwrif.org/29/high-school-interns

If you or someone you know is still a junior or senior in high school and is interested in medicine, the **MAGEE-WOMENS RESEARCH INSTITUTE INTERNSHIP** is the thing to do. Not only can you get published at the end of the program, but you also get *paid* for your time there. Heck, yes.

the-synapse-project.org

Founded and directed by two 17-year-old heroines, **THE SYNAPSE PROJECT** uses information and mentorship to encourage women to get into neuroscience. On their site, you can learn all about the brain and current developments in neuroscience. And if you dig it, you can network for some cool internships and jobs.

amwa-doc.org

Anyone can become a member of the **AMERICAN WOMEN'S MEDICAL ASSOCIATION**, whether you're a physician, resident, medical student, pre-med student, health care professional, or even just a supporter of women in medicine. Founded in 1915, AMWA fights for improvements for women in medical science, and it's pretty darn awesome all-round.

Espionage

womeninhomelandsecurity.com

Obviously, becoming a spy is not *quite* as simple as Googling "how to become a spy." **WOMEN IN HOMELAND SECURITY** is a nonprofit with over 3,000 members that teaches ladies about what it takes to prevent incidents in the United States on the local, state, and federal levels. They even have a book club!

learncryptography.com

Interested in ciphers and codes? **LEARN CRYPTOGRAPHY** can teach you everything from cryptanalysis to hash functions to encryption. Start with the Playfair Cipher and use it to pass notes to your friends, who will never be able to figure out what they say and will probably never speak to you again but *totally worth it*.

stilettospyschool.com

If you happen to find yourself in New York City or Las Vegas, head for a mission at the **STILETTO SPY SCHOOL**! Inspired by bad babes like Emma Peel, Lara Croft, Charlie's Angels, and Sidney Bristow, you can turn yourself into an IRL Bond Girl with skills like hand-to-hand combat, knife fighting, awareness training, stunt driving, dancing, even poker and pool—all from Special Forces and military-trained instructors.

duolingo.com

All the best spies know more than one language. Teach yourself a new one for free with **DUOLINGO**, which currently offers lessons online in a *ton* of different European languages, as well as a smartphone app for studying on the go.

onpointtactical.com

Want to learn skills like Escape and Evasion, Urban Survival, or Off-Grid Medical Care? Sign up for a class at **ONPOINT TACTICAL**, offered all across America. Though the company originally catered to the military and law enforcement organizations, they now have courses for civilians looking to up their survival skills game. That's how you know it's legit.

Exploration and Adventure

women.nasa.gov/outreach-programs/

If you dream about captaining your own awesome ship in space and encountering a bunch of friendly aliens, **WOMEN@NASA** can help you do the next best thing. They have programs for gals of all ages (like NASA SISTER and Aspire to Inspire) that encourage all ladies to get involved in SPACE.

exxpedition.com

If you want to really get your science explorer on, you should join an **EXXPEDITION**, a series of all-women voyages focusing on gathering data about the harmful effects of toxins in our environment. Heading everywhere from Norway to the Amazon, Exxpeditions need women with all different kinds of skills, from sailors to cooks to scientists to filmmakers.

fosterscholars.noaa.gov

This graduate scholarship from the **NATIONAL OCEANIC AND ATMOSPHERIC ADMINISTRATION** is all about encouraging women and other marginalized groups to pursue independent scholarship in oceanography, marine biology, and maritime archaeology (which sounds like *the actual best career*). The scholarship can land you way over a living wage, plus a paid collaboration at an NOAA facility.

browngirlsfly.com

BROWN GIRLS FLY is a "melanin-infused perspective on travel" that's all about what it's like to be a woman while "traveling Brown." Founded by sisters Chelle and Crystal Roberts, the site hosts women of color writing all kinds of interesting articles on being ex-pats in different countries, what it's like to travel alone as a Black woman in China, and even what to pack before traveling while being not white.

seap.asee.org

The **SCIENCE AND ENGINEERING APPRENTICESHIP PROGRAM** sends high school students to Department of Navy labs all over the United States for the chance to learn more about their STEM field of choice. Working with badasses from the Navy *and* getting to travel while still in high school, all for the sake of higher learning in science? Sign me up.

Selected Bibliography

For a complete list of references consulted, including primary
sources, visit quirkbooks.com/book/wonder-women.

Wang Zhenyi

Leung, Angela Ki Che. "Wang Zhenyi." *Biographical Dictionary of Chinese Women*. Vol 1, *The Qing Period, 1644–1911*. Ed. Lily Xiao Hong Lee, Clara Lau, and A. D. Stefanowska. Trans. W. Zhang. New York: Routledge, 2015.

Ogilvie, Marilyn, and Joy Harvey, eds. "Wang Zhenyi (Chen-i)." *The Biographical Dictionary of Women in Science: Pioneering Lives from Ancient Times to the Mid-20th Century*. New York: Routledge, 2003.

Peterson, Barbara Bennett, ed. "Wang Zhenyi." In *Notable Women of China: Shang Dynasty to the Early Twentieth Century*. New York: Routledge, 2000. [*epigraph source*]

Ada Lovelace

Essinger, James. *Ada's Algorithm: How Lord Byron's Daughter Ada Lovelace Launched the Digital Age through the Poetry of Numbers*. London: Gibson Square Books, 2013. [*epigraph source*]

Moore, Doris Langley. *Ada, Countess of Lovelace: Byron's Legitimate Daughter*. New York: Harper & Row, 1977.

Stein, Dorothy. *Ada: A Life and Legacy*. Cambridge: MIT Press, 1987.

Woolley, Benjamin. *The Bride of Science: Romance, Reason, and Byron's Daughter*. New York: McGraw-Hill, 2000.

Lise Meitner

Hahn, Otto. "From the Natural Transmutations of Uranium to Its Artificial Fission." Nobel Lecture, Dec. 13, 1946. Web.

L'Annunziata, Michael F. *Radioactivity: Introduction and History*, 224–36. Oxford, UK: Elsevier, 2007. [*epigraph source*]

Meitner, Lise. "The Status of Women in the Professions." *Physics Today* 13, no. 8 (1960): 16–21.

———. "Looking Back." *Bulletin of the Atomic Sciences*, Nov. 1964, 2–7.

Rife, Patricia. *Lise Meitner and the Dawn of the Nuclear Age*. Boston: Birkhäuser, 1999.

Sime, Ruth Lewin. *Lise Meitner: A Life in Physics*. Berkeley: University of California Press, 1996.

Emmy Noether

Byers, Nina. "Emmy Noether (1882–1935)." In *Out of the Shadows: Contributions of Twentieth-Century Women to Physics*. Ed.Nina Byers and Gary Williams, 86–96. Cambridge: Cambridge University Press, 2006.

Dick, Auguste. *Emmy Noether, 1882–1935*. Trans.H. I. Blocher. Boston: Birkhäuser, 1981. [*epigraph source*]

Einstein, Albert. "The Late Emmy Noether." *New York Times*, May 4, 1935, 12.

Huylebrouck, Dirk, and Alice Silverberg. "Emmy Noether in Erlangen." *Mathematical Intelligencer* 23, no. 3 (2001): 44–49.

Osen, Lynn M. *Women in Mathematics*. Cambridge: MIT Press, 1975.

Alice Ball

Epigraph source: Text of the memorial plaque commemorating Ball's achievements at the University of Hawai'i at Mānoa

Ball, Alice A., and William M. Dehn. "Benzoylations in Ether Solution." *Journal of the American Chemical Society* 36, no. 10 (1914): 2091–2101.

Brown, Jeannette. *African American Women Chemists*. New York: Oxford University Press, 2011.

"Graduates of College of Hawaii Get Good Positions as Soon as They Leave School." *Honolulu Star-Bulletin*, Jun. 2, 1915, 3.

Wermager, Paul. "Healing the Sick." In *They Followed the Trade Winds: African Americans in Hawai'i*. Edited by Miles M. Jackson, 168–74. Honolulu: University of Hawai'i at Mānoa, Dept. of Sociology, 2004.

Jacqueline Felice de Almania

Amt, Emilie. *Women's Lives in Medieval Europe: A Sourcebook*. 2d ed. New York: Routledge, 2010. [*epigraph source*]

Ehrenreich, Barbara, and Deirdre English. *Witches, Midwives & Nurses: A History of Women Healers*. New York: Feminist Press at CUNY, 2010.

Herlihy, David. *Opera Muliebria: Women and Work in Medieval Europe*. New York: McGraw-Hill, 1990.

Hughes, Muriel Joy. *Women Healers in Medieval Life and Literature*. New York: King's Crown Press, 1943.

Emily and Elizabeth Blackwell

"An M.D. in a Gown." Punch 16 (1849): 226.

Blackwell, Elizabeth. *The Influence of Women in the Profession of Medicine*. Baltimore, 1890.

Blackwell, Elizabeth, and Emily Blackwell, *Address on the Medical Education of Women*. New York: Baptist & Taylor, 1864. [*epigraph source*]

D. K. "The Late Medical Degree to a Female." *Boston Medical and Surgical Journal* 40 (1849): 58–59.

Faderman, Lillian. *To Believe in Women: What Lesbians Have Done for America—A History*. Boston: Houghton-Mifflin, 1999.

Wilson, Dorothy Clarke. *Lone Woman: The Story of Elizabeth Blackwell, the First Woman Doctor*. Boston: Little Brown, 1970.

Ogino Ginko

Hastings, Sally Ann. "Women's Professional Expertise and Women's Suffrage in Japan, 1868–1952." In *Gender State and Nation in Modern Japan*. Ed. Andrea Germer, Vera Mackie, and Ulrike Wöhr. New York: Routledge, 2014.

Lublin, Elizabeth Dorn. *Reforming Japan: The Woman's Christian Temperance Union in the Meiji Period*. Vancouver: University of British Columbia Press, 2010.

Nakamura, Ellen. "Ogino Ginko's Vision: 'The Past and Future of Women Doctors in Japan' (1893)." *U.S.-Japan Women's Journal* 34 (2008): 3–18. [*epigraph source*]

Ogino, Ginko. "Experiences of the First Woman Physician in Modern Japan." *Japan Evangelist* 1, no. 2 (1893): 88–91.

———. "The Past and Present of Japanese Woman Physicians." Translated by Nakamura Chonosuke. *Japan Evangelist* 1, no. 4 (1894): 209–11.

Anandibai Joshi

Epigraph: Letter from A. Joshi to Alfred Jones, Jun 28, 1883. Archives & Special Collections on Women in Medicine & Homeopathy, Drexel University College of Medicine, Philadelphia, PA.

Dell, Caroline Healey. *The Life of Anandabai Joshee, a Kinswoman of the Pundita Ramabai.* Boston: Roberts Brothers, 1888. Web.

Gurjarpadhye, Prachi. "Through a Changing Feminist Lens: Three Biographies of Anandibai Joshi." *Economic and Political Weekly* 49, no. 33 (2014): 37–40.

"The Hindoo Woman at the Medical College." Daily Enterprise (Livingston, MT), May 10, 1884.

Joshee, Anandibai. *Obstetrics among the Aryan Hindoos.* PhD diss., Women's Medical College of Pennsylvania, 1886. Drexel University College of Medicine Archives. Web.

Kosambi, Meera. "Anandibai Joshee: Retrieving a Fragmented Feminist Image." *Economic and Political Weekly* 31, no. 49 (1996): 3189–97.

Marie Equi

"OB Taylor Horse Whipped." *Dalles Times-Mountaineer,* Jul. 22, 1893.

"Dr. Equi Stabs Officer." *Morning Oregonian,* Jul. 18, 1913, p. 5. [*epigraph source*]

Cook, Tom. "Radical Politics, Radical Love: The Life of Dr. Marie Equi." *Northwest Gay and Lesbian History* 1, nos. 3 and 4 (1996 and 1997). Web.

Helquist, Michael. *Marie Equi: Radical Politics and Outlaw Passions.* Corvallis: Oregon State University Press, 2015.

Krieger, Nancy. "Queen of the Bolsheviks: The Hidden History of Dr. Marie Equi." *Radical America* 17, no. 5 (1983): 55–73.

Brita Tott

Epigraph: Latin inscription from the Ösmo chapel mural commissioned by Tott.

Bruun, Henry, and Thelma Jexlev. "Birgitte Olufsdatter Thott." *Den Store Danske Encyklopædi* (The Great Danish Encyclopedia). From the Danish Biographical Lexicon, 3d ed., 1984.

Fryxell, Anders. *The History of Sweden.* Vol. 1. Trans. Anne von Schoultz. Richard Bentley, 1844.

Jørkov, Birgitte. "Birgitte Thott (- efter 1498) Thott, Birgitte Olufsdatter."

Dansk kvindebiografisk leksikon (Danish Female Biographical Dictionary). KVINFO, 2003.

Rystad, Göran. "Falskt och äkta i Hammerstaaffären." *Scandia: Tidskrift för historisk forskning* (Magazine for Historical Research*)* 25, no. 1 (1959): 108–12.

—————————— **Mary Bowser** ——————————

"The Adventures of a Government Female Spy." *Brooklyn Eagle*, Sep. 25, 1865.

Beymer, William Gilmore. "Miss Van Lew." *Harper's* 123 (Jun. 1, 1911): 86.

Leveen, Lois. "The Spy Photo That Fooled NPR, the U.S. Army Intelligence Center, and Me." *Atlantic*, Jun. 27, 2013.

———. "A Black Spy in the Confederate White House." *New York Times*, Jun. 21, 2012. [*epigraph source*]

Sizer, Lyde Cullen. "Bowser, Mary Elizabeth." In *African American Lives*. Ed. Henry Louis Gates Jr. and Evelyn Brooks Higginbotham, 92–93. New York: Oxford University Press, 2004.

Winkler, H. Donald. *Stealing Secrets: How a Few Daring Women Deceived Generals, Impacted Battles, and Altered the Course of the Civil War.* New York: Sourcebooks, 2010.

Varon, Elizabeth R. Southern Lady, Yankee Spy: *The True Story of Elizabeth Van Lew, a Union Agent in the Heart of the Confederacy.* Cambridge: Oxford University Press, 2003.

—————————— **Sarah Emma Edmonds** ——————————

"A Female Soldier Is Pensioned." *Winfield Courier*, Apr. 3, 1884. [*epigraph source*]

Edmonds, S. Emma E. *Nurse and Spy in the Union Army.* Hartford, CT: W. S. Williams & Co., 1865.

Eggleston, Larry G. *Women in the Civil War: Extraordinary Stories of Soldiers, Spies, Nurses, Doctors, Crusaders, and Others.* Jefferson, NC: McFarland, 2013.

Gansler, Laura Leedy. *The Mysterious Private Thompson: The Double Life of Sarah Emma Edmonds, Civil War Soldier.* Lincoln: University of Nebraska Press, 2007.

Tsui, Bonnie. *She Went to the Field: Women Soldiers of the Civil War.* Guilford, CT: Globe Pequot, 2006.

──────── **Elvira Chaudoir** ────────

Crowdy, Terry. *Deceiving Hitler: Double Cross and Deception in World War II*. Oxford, UK: Osprey Publishing, 2008.

Macintyre, Ben. *Ben Macintyre's Espionage Files: Agent Zigzag, Operation Mincemeat & Double Cross*. London: A&C Black, 2012.

───. *Double Cross: The True Story of the D-Day Spies*. New York: Crown/Archetype, 2012. [*epigraph source*]

West, Nigel. *The Guy Liddell Diaries Vol. II: 1942–1945: MI5's Director of Counter-Espionage in World War II*. New York: Routledge, 2007.

──────── **Noor Inayat Khan** ────────

Basu, Shrabani. *Spy Princess: The Life of Noor Inayat Khan*. Omega, 2007.

Fuller, Jean Overton. *Madeleine: Noor-un-nisa Inayat Khan*. Rotterdam: East-West Publications, 1988.

Khan, Noor Inayat. *Twenty Jataka Tales*. 1939. Reprint. Rochester, VT: Inner Traditions, 1985. [*epigraph source*]

Talwar, Divya. "Churchill's Asian Spy Princess Comes Out of the Shadows." *BBC News*, Jan. 11, 2011. Web.

──────── **Huang Daopo** ────────

Bray, Francesca. *Technology and Gender: Fabrics of Power in Late Imperial China*, 215. Berkeley: University of California Press, 1997.

Meschel, Susan V. "Huang Daopo." In *Routledge International Encyclopedia of Women: Global Women's Issues and Knowledge*. Ed. Cheris Kramarae and Dale Spender, 1783–84. London: Routledge, 2004.

Xu, Shidua. "Huang *daopo*." *Biographical Dictionary of Chinese Women*. Vol. 2, *Tang Through Ming, 618–1644*. Trans. Michael Paton. Ed. Lily Xiao Hong Lee and Sue Wiles, 140–42. London: Routledge, 2015. [*epigraph source*]

Zurndorfer, Harriet T. "Cotton Textile Manufacture and Marketing in Late Imperial China and the 'Great Divergence.'" *Journal of the Economic & Social History of the Orient* 54, no. 5 (2011): 701–38.

──────── **Margaret Knight** ────────

Hanaford, Phebe A. *Daughters of America; or, Women of the Century*. Augusta, ME: True & Co., 1883. [*epigraph source*]

Macdonald, Anne. *Feminine Ingenuity: How Women Inventors Changed America*. New York: Random House, 1994.

Penny, Virginia. *The Employments of Women: A Cyclopaedia of Woman's Work*. Boston: Walker, Wise, & Co., 1863.

"She Was a Notable Woman." *Framingham Evening News*, Oct. 13, 1914.

Stanley, Autumn. *Mothers and Daughters of Invention: Notes for a Revised History of Technology*. New Brunswick, NJ: Rutgers University Press, 1995.

"Woman Inventor of Sleeve Valve Motor." *New York Sun*, Mar. 24, 1912, 10.

Miriam Benjamin

"Gets Pay at Last." *Boston Daily Globe*, May 20, 1906, 9.

"Estate of Samuel Lee." *Congressional Record Containing the Proceedings and Debates of the Fifty-Ninth Congress, First Session, Also Special Session of the Senate*. Vol. 40. Washington, D.C.: Government Printing Office, 1906. Pg. 3298.

Miriam Benjamin's "Gong and Signal Chair for Hotels, &c." US Patent No. 386,289. Jul. 17, 1888. [*epigraph source*]

"Miss Miriam E. Benjamin. *The Bee* (Washington D.C.), Jul. 19, 1884, 3.

Stanley, Autumn. *Mothers and Daughters of Invention: Notes for a Revised History of Technology*. New Brunswick, NJ: Rutgers University Press, 1995.

Bessie Blount Griffin

"A Woman and an Idea: French Officials Accept Gift of N. J. Inventor." *Afro-American Magazine*, Sep. 6, 1952. [*epigraph source*]

Carter, Art, "Automatic Invalid Feeder: Jerseyan Gives Invention to French Government." *Afro-American Magazine*, Nov. 10, 1951, 22.

Sluby, Patricia Carter. *The Inventive Spirit of African Americans: Patented Ingenuity*. Westport, CT: Praeger, 2004.

Stanley, Autumn. *Mothers and Daughters of Invention: Notes for a Revised History of Technology*. New Brunswick, NJ: Rutgers University Press, 1995.

Thomas, James, Jr. "Former Diggs Chapel student tries to preserve school's memory." *Virginian-Pilot*, Sep. 9, 2008.

Mary Sherman Morgan

Ellis, Barbara, and Michael Rogers. "Rocket Girl to Premiere on Seminar Day." *Caltech News, California Institute of Technology* 42, no. 1 (2008): 15.

Kraemer, Robert S., and Vince Wheelock. *Rocketdyne: Powering Humans into Space*. Reston, VA: American Institute of Aeronautics and Astronautics, 2006.

Morgan, George D. *Rocket Girl: The Story of Mary Sherman Morgan, America's First Female Rocket Scientist*. Amherst, NY: Prometheus Books, 2013. [*epigraph source*]

Maria Sibylla Merian

Davis, Natalie Zemon Davis. *Women on the Margins: Three Seventeenth-Century Lives*. Cambridge: Harvard University Press, 1995.

Etheridge, Kay. "Maria Sibylla Merian's Frogs." *Bibliotheca Herpetologica* 8, no. 2 (2010): 20–27.

Freedburg, David. "Science, Commerce, and Art: Neglected Topics at the Junction of History and Art History." In *Art in History, History in Art: Studies in Seventeenth-Century Dutch Culture*. Santa Monica, CA: The Getty Center for the History of Art and the Humanities, 1991. [*epigraph source*]

Todd, Kim. *Chrysalis: Maria Sibylla Merian and the Secrets of Metamorphosis*. Orlando, FL: Harcourt, 2007.

Ulenberg, Sandrine. *Maria Sibylla Merian and Daughters: Women of Art and Science*. Amsterdam: The Rembrandt House Museum, 2008.

Annie Smith Peck

Jordan, Elizabeth. "Annie Peck and Popocatepetl." New Yorker, Oct. 3, 1936, 41.

"Miss Peck Goes Out to Climb the Heights." *New York Times*, Jun 3, 1911. [*epigraph source*]

Miller, Dorcas S. *Adventurous Women: The Inspiring Lives of Nine Early Outdoorswomen*. Boulder, CO: Pruett Publishing, 2000.

Olds, Elizabeth Fagg. *Women of the Four Winds: The Adventures of Four of America's First Women Explorers*. New York: Mariner Books, 1999.

Peck, Annie S. *The South American Tour*. New York: George H. Doran, 1913.

Ynes Mexia

Bonta, Marcia Myers. *American Women Afield: Writings by Pioneering Women Naturalists.* College Station: Texas A&M University Press, 1995.

Bracelin, N. Floy. "Ynes Mexia." *Science* 88, no. 2295 (1938): 586.

Mexia, Ynes. "Three Thousand Miles up the Amazon." *Sierra Club Bulletin* 18 (1933): 88.

Moore, Patricia Ann. "Cultivating Science in the Field: Alice Eastwood, Ynes Mexia and California Botany, 1890–1940." PhD diss., University of California, Los Angeles, 1996.

Ross, Michael Elsohn. *A World of Her Own: 24 Amazing Women Explorers and Adventurers.* Chicago: Chicago Review Press, 2014.

Mexia, Ynes. "Camping on the Equator." *Sierra Club Bulletin* 22 (1937): 85. [*epigraph source*]

Annie Londonderry

"A Whirl 'Round the World." *Omaha World Herald*, Aug 25 1895.

"Bloomers Abhorred." *Iowa State Register*, Sep 7, 1895.

"Champion of Her Sex." *New York Sunday World*, Feb 2, 1896.

"Mrs. Stanton Likes Bloomers." *Rocky Mountain News*, Aug 11, 1895.

Zheutlin, Peter. "Chasing Annie." *Bicycling*, May 2005: 64–69. [*epigraph source*]

———. *Around the World on Two Wheels: Annie Londonderry's Extraordinary Ride.* New York: Citadel, 2008.

Bessie Coleman

Beeman, Cynthia J., and Dan K. Utley. *History Ahead: Stories Beyond the Texas Roadside Markers.* College Station: Texas A&M University Press, 2010. [*epigraph source*]

Broadnax, Samuel L. *Blue Skies, Black Wings: African American Pioneers of Aviation.* Westport, CT: Praeger, 2007.

"Negress Pilots Airplane." *New York Times*, Sep. 4, 1922.

Rich, Doris L. *Queen Bess: Daredevil Aviator.* Washington, DC: Smithsonian Institute Press, 1993.

"They Take to the Sky." *Ebony* 32, no. 7 (1977): 87–96.

Index

Acknowledgments

Thank you to my editrix extraordinaire, Blair Thornburgh, for believing both in me and in this book. You are *so* good at your job, it blows my mind. You always had a vision for *Wonder Women*, and you helped refine it into that sweet spot somewhere between textbook and Tumblr. Thank you for making me sound like a better writer than I am.

I don't know where I would be were it not for my intrepid and incredible agent, Maria Vicente. There's no one I'd rather take this journey with than you, my beautiful, Buffy-loving babe. You're a saint for handling all my late-night texts and feelings and junk. Let's do this again sometime.

Jason, Brett, Nicole, Mary Ellen, Julie, Kelsey, and the whole team over at Quirk Books—I am so grateful and proud to be part of this publishing family. Thank you for actually wanting to work with me *again*. And to Anne and the Penguin Random House Canada gang up here in the Kingdom of the North—you're stuck with me again! Muahaha. (Seriously, though, you're the best. Thanks for everything).

A *massive* thank you to the University of Western Ontario (especially Professor M!); the Toronto Reference Library; Stanford's Hoover Archives; the University of Oregon Library; the Boston Public Library; Diane Chang at the University of Hawai'i Manoa; and Christina Sandquist-Öberg.

I can't say thank you enough to illustrator Sophia Foster-Dimino and designer Andie Reid, who brought my li'l manuscript to life with their incredible visual skills. I am so lucky to be able to work with brilliant women like you.

ACKNOWLEDGMENTS

Thanks to the fine folks at BioWare for getting me through book brain drain with *Dragon Age: Inquisition* (especially Ritzy, Patrick, Mae, Mike, and the rest of the usual DAIMP suspects), and to everyone involved with making *Supernatural;* if there is a better show to edit a book to, I have yet to find it. Thanks too to Christine and the Rosedale Starbucks for all the black tea lemonades (sweetened).

Mom and Dad, thank you for never telling me to get a *real* degree or a *real* master's or a *real* job, and for encouraging me to be weird and geeky and introverted. Thanks to my dad for feeding my desire to write with my first laptop way back when, and to my mom for copyediting literally everything I've ever written. Love you.

And, of course, the final and biggest thank you of all is for my partner in crime through the writing of this book, Teddy Wilson. Your sandwich deliveries kept me going when I was feeling down; your advice, my compass when I was feeling directionless; and your kindness, better for me than even the tastiest of pastries (which is saying something, coming from me). Thanks for not throwing away my Dean Winchester body pillow (yet).

Oh, and thank you to *you*, babely reader. Now get out there and kick some butts.